M000297446

THE
DOG LOVER'S
POCKET BIBLE

THE
DOG LOVER'S
POCKET BIBLE

MALINI ROY
WITH HOLLY IVINS

This edition first published in Great Britain 2009 by
Crimson Publishing, a division of Crimson Business Ltd
Westminster House
Kew Road
Richmond
Surrey
TW9 2ND

A catalogue record for this book is available from the British Library.

ISBN 978 1 907087 03 5

Printed and bound by LegoPrint SpA, Trento.

CONTENTS

INTRODUCTION

Did you know that dogs are better at reading our body language than chimpanzees? Did you ever wonder where the phrase 'dog days' came from? Have you ever wanted to know the difference between a working dog and a toy dog? Do you often wonder why dogs are such an integral part of our lives? Or perhaps you are looking to become one of the millions of dog owners in the world? Then the *Dog Lover's Pocket Bible* is for you.

Dogs have had a relationship with man since ancient times, and from cave paintings in Spain made over 12,000 years ago, to the lovable characters of Snoopy and Gromit, today's, dogs are an integral part of our culture and society. Dogs are not only lovable pets but have played a useful role in our lives; helping man hunt, to herd cattle, and even acting as a guide dog for the blind: dogs truly have earned the title of man's best friend.

This book is both a source of useful information on the history and trivia of dogs, as well as a practical 'owner's manual' providing advice, hints and tips on everything involved in owning a dog, from choosing a breed to deciding on a name, to what to feed your dog and what type of training you want to do.

The *Dog Lover's Pocket Bible* will help you understand our love affair with dogs and to become a truly great owner. As the 19th century author George Eliot put it, a dog offers love 'altogether ignorant of our faults' – unlike many humans. At the very least, your significant other will scold you if you've been out late. But a dog is happy to see you, wherever, whenever. Dogs have been man's best friend for thousands of years and if you put in the right amount of commitment and love you'll end up with a loving and loyal part of the family.

ALL ABOUT DOGS

🐕 WHY OWN A DOG? 🐕

Aside from the undying loyalty and love you can get from having a dog as a pet, there are a number of other benefits to being a dog owner:

- There are health benefits to be had from walking a dog. Walking helps you both keep lean and fit, and encounter other dog owners, allowing you more social interaction.

- Recent studies have shown that people who own a pet generally have less chance of having a heart attack.

- A dog is good for your emotional well being – a fact supported by scientific research.

Pocket fact 🐾

AIDS patients who owned a dog were found to be less likely to suffer from depression. Studies have also shown that patients who are in contact with dogs after hospital treatment or illness have a faster recovery time.

🐕 HOW THE DOG GOT ITS NAME 🐕

It is unclear what the exact origins of the word 'dog' are, but there is a strong argument to suggest that it comes from an Old English word *docga*, which means a 'powerful breed of canine'. The word docga is said to derive from the Germanic term, *dukkon*, which translates as 'finger muscle' – perhaps an indication of the dog's earliest role as a worker.

Correspondingly the word 'hound' comes from a Proto-Indo-European word, which follows an indirect root from the Latin word *canis*, meaning dog.

Pocket fact 🐾

The dog was given the Latin name Canis familiaris *and* Canis familiarus domesticus *in 1758.*

Recently the Smithsonian Institution and the American Society of Mammalogists have reclassified the dog as Canis lupus familiaris, *a sub-species of the grey wolf* Canis lupus.

🐈 DOGS THROUGH THE AGES 🐈

It is widely agreed that today's modern dog evolved from a small pack of wolves tamed by humans living in China some 15,000 years ago. Scientists have recently published findings which suggest that all modern dog breeds are descended from just three she-wolves. However, other scientists argue that some dogs also contain DNA similar to coyotes and jackals, which must, at some point, have contributed to their development.

It is thought that as pack animals the wolves would be drawn to cave-dwelling humans for companionship and warmth. In return, the humans discovered that the wolves were highly skilled at hunting and used these skills to their advantage. The early humans also used dogs to guard their settlements.

It is dogs' relationship with humans throughout the ages which has shaped and created the modern dog we know and love today.

Mythical wolves

The relationship between ancient man and wolves appears in many foundation myths, such as the story of Romulus and Remus, the brothers who, according to Roman mythology, founded the ancient city of Rome. Romulus and Remus were abandoned as babies and were saved when they were suckled by a she-wolf.

Wolves have also appeared in Turkic, Norse and Native American mythology, and in Japan, farmers would leave offerings to wolf shrines in a plea for them to protect their crops.

SELECTIVE BREEDING BEGINS

As ancient man began to domesticate the dog he also began the process which led to the large number of modern breeds of dog that we have today. By choosing dogs based on their hunting skills, their ability to pull sleds and their usefulness as guards (for both humans and livestock), ancient man created the first working dogs. It was this working relationship which led to the domestication of dogs, the creation of their various breeds, and eventually their adoption as pets.

Dogs are classified by their breed but often also by their 'group' (see p.32). They were initially tamed to be working animals, not pets. Even the possible origins of the word dog, a Germanic term 'dukkon', which means 'finger muscle', hints at the valuable working role dogs played in ancient man's life. So how did these working animals make the leap to being man's best friend?

Some crucial moments in the evolution of the modern dog

- *30,000BC: archaeological evidence of the earliest possible domestication of a dog.*
- *7,000BC: archaeological evidence definitively proving domestication of a dog.*
- *By the beginning of the Bronze Age (c. 4,500 BC), there are fossil remains of a few kinds of dogs that are recognisable as the modern breeds of mastiffs and sight hounds (like the Greyhound or Saluki).*

BECOMING MAN'S BEST FRIEND

Although most dogs were selected for their skills in different practical tasks there were instances of dogs being chosen for their companionship and loyalty.

In ancient Rome some dogs escaped work by being adopted as pets by wealthy Roman women. Their warmth was supposed to cure stomach ache, and their beauty was extolled. Lapdogs have become a common accessory of the wealthy socialite ever since, even appearing as the Chihuahua companions of socialites like Paris Hilton today. As history and industry progressed, there was less and less work for dogs to do – and so they gradually became pets instead.

Pocket fact 🐾

Two of the survivors from the Titanic were dogs – a Pekinese and a Pomeranian.

THEIR ROLE TODAY

Dogs still strike a balance between being practical working dogs (whether they are guide dogs or police sniffer dogs) and lovable pets. Most of the estimated 400 million dogs in the world today are kept as pets and no longer fulfil their intended purpose. However, the relationship between man and dog looks set to continue as strong as ever.

Pocket fact ❧

Dogs have been proven to be better at reading signals from humans than our closest genetic relative, the chimpanzee. When faced with food hidden beneath buckets, dogs were found to be the best at following signals and hints from people in the room. This skill was also found in the puppies tested, proving it to be an instinctive and not a learned behaviour.

🐕 A DOG'S PHYSIQUE 🐕

There are a few distinguishing features which make up man's best friend. There may be more than 400 species of dogs in all kinds of shapes and sizes but here is a rundown of a few of their shared features.

Pocket fact ❧

Dogs, taken together as a species — pet, stray or wild — make up 400 million bodies on the planet. Of these, about 7.3 million live in the UK.

EYES

- Dogs, like their owners, have binocular vision, although they are unable to perceive as much detail as humans. Some breeds, such as hunting dogs, have a wider field of vision than humans, while breeds with deeper-set eyes have a narrower field of vision.

- Dogs are also less able to notice stationary items; they recognise items by movement and rely heavily on their sense of smell to perceive the world around them. Their vision is very sensitive to movement, a trait which has developed from their hunting instincts.

- Contrary to popular belief, dogs are not colour blind but they do have a limited range of colours which they can see. They have two types of colour receptors (cones) instead of three like humans. Most colours that humans can see are a combination of red, blue, and yellow. Remove one of these colours, and that is what dogs see. So the colours green, yellow, and orange look pretty much the same to a dog.

- Most dogs have brown eyes but a few have blue eyes.

- Dogs have a third eyelid to protect their eye from dirt and dust.

EARS AND HEARING

- It is a well known fact that dogs have superior hearing to humans, and to most of the animal kingdom.

- Their hearing range is 40Hz to 60,000Hz, which means it extends far beyond their owners' at both ends of the spectrum.

- They are able to move their ears, meaning they have a greater ability to pinpoint sounds. The curved or cupped shape of a dog's ear also helps.

- Dogs are able to hear sounds at a distance four times further away than humans.

- Dogs have an incredible ability to distinguish individual sounds, allowing them to recognise danger or even their owner's footsteps.

Pocket fact ❧

Many of us are familiar with guide dogs, who offer independence and guidance to the visually impaired, but since the 1980s hearing dogs have offered this same invaluable help to those who are hearing impaired.

TONGUE AND TASTE

- Some owners will tell you that dogs will eat anything, which could be due to the fact that they only have 1,700 taste buds, while humans have about 9,000.

- Dogs have been known to have food preferences and avoid certain foods, suggesting they are able to distinguish flavours. This aversion to certain types of food is an instinctive trait and so dogs will avoid any food which makes them ill.

Pocket fact ❧

There are two breeds of dog with black tongues instead of pink: the Chow Chow and the Shar-Pei.

- Like babies, puppies are born without teeth. Throughout their life they will grow and lose baby teeth until they end up with a full set of 42 adult teeth.

- Dogs need to chew bones or toys to keep their teeth healthy. It will also satisfy their innate behaviour and should stop them chewing other things, like shoes.

Pocket fact 🐾

Dogs pant to regulate their body temperature. Panting allows them to quickly cool down their tongue and mouth and cools the major blood vessels leading to the head. They need to pant as they have fewer sweat glands than humans. Their sweat glands are actually in the pads of their paws.

NOSE AND SNIFFING

- Dogs have around 220 million scent receptors (compared to five million in humans) and are able to distinguish individual smells among a variety.

- It is thought that dogs can distinguish two types of scent: an air scent (created in the air by a passing object or person) and a ground scent (which remains detectable for much longer).

- Dogs are able to perceive the slightest changes in atmosphere and can even detect changes in those around them, such as hormonal changes or increased sweating.

- Dogs have been used for their sense of smell for centuries, from hunting dogs to sniffer dogs detecting drugs, tracking down missing people and even identifying endangered bumblebees.

Pocket fact 🐾

Trained dogs are known for their ability to track down missing people but a BBC documentary actually showed that some dogs are able to sniff out cancer in their owners. While there is still a lot of speculation around this subject there is further research being done into the practical applications.

🐕 HOW LONG DOES A DOG LIVE? 🐈

On average, a dog lives for about 12 to 14 years. It's said that one dog year is equivalent to seven human years.

FINDING OUT THE AGE OF A DOG

To find out the age of a dog, look at its teeth. For a puppy, you can look at the stage of growth to establish its age. For an adult dog, you look at the wear of the teeth instead (bear in mind that the wear will depend on the level of dental care the dog receives). As a general guide:

- Look at the front four teeth in the upper jaw. Dogs have a visible mark on these teeth which doesn't disappear until they are six years old.

- Heavy plaque build-up and missing teeth will suggest an older dog of 10 to 15 years.

The table below gives a comparison of a dog's age with human years. Keep in mind that this is isn't written in stone – diet, health and exercise will make a lot of difference to how long a dog lives.

Human years	1	2	3	4	5	6	7	8	9	10	11	12	13	14	15
Small breeds	15	24	28	32	36	40	44	48	52	56	60	64	68	72	76
Medium breeds	15	24	28	32	36	42	47	51	56	60	65	69	74	78	83
Large breeds	15	24	28	32	36	45	50	55	61	66	72	77	82	88	93

KEY

Puppy

Adult

Elderly

Pocket fact 🐾

The world's oldest dog is said to have been an Australian Cattle Dog called Bluey, who lived to the age of 29 years 5 months. You have to take this with a pinch of salt though, as the record hasn't been verified. A surer record is that of Bramble, a Collie from Somerset, who lived to at least the age of 27 on a vegetarian diet.

🐕 BREEDS OF DOG 🐈

The reason we see dogs in so many shapes, sizes and colours (and temperaments) is because of selective breeding. Dogs with desirable traits are mated generation after generation to establish a particular breed.

Breeding in this way started with the beginning of the domestic dog, as man bred dogs which proved to be good at protection and hunting – and naturally weeded out the less useful dogs. Breeding

ALL ABOUT DOGS • 11

continues today in the creation of designer breeds such as the Labradoodle (a Labrador/Poodle mix) and the Puggle (a Pug/Beagle mix).

How many breeds exist?

In the UK, the Kennel Club recognises 209 breeds, of which 75% are pedigree, 11% are crossbreeds and 14% are mixed breeds. Different countries have their own lists of certified breeds, depending on the make up of the dog population in the country.

PUREBRED

Purebred dogs will be one specific breed. These modern dogs' ancestry is known from documented evidence. A dog with a pedigree will have a family tree showing a list of sires and dams to prove its lineage.

In human terms, pedigree dogs are the old-style aristocrats of the doggy world, carefully preserved with certain traits.

A purebred might be more predictable in personality and habits. President Obama's Portuguese Water Dog (or PWD), for example, is known to be suitable for children with allergies.

Pocket fact ❧

A purebred generally costs more than other breeds. Its price can be anywhere between £800 and £1,500.

CROSSBREED

'What do you get when you cross a Cocker Spaniel and a Poodle? A Cockerpoo'

No, that isn't a joke. The Cockerpoo is a real crossbreed: a planned mating between two purebreds. Crossbred dogs have a greater gene pool than purebreds, which means they can be less susceptible to inherited diseases.

DESIGNER DOGS

Perhaps your dream dog is a Poodle but you're allergic to dog hair; in that case a Labradoodle could be the perfect dog for you. 'Designer dogs' are those which have been bred to fit the exclusive tastes of the owner, be it for practical or aesthetic reasons.

Designer dogs have been around since the 1990s. That's why nowadays there are as many diverse breeds as the Cockerpoo (Cocker Spaniel x Poodle), the Goldendoodle (Golden Retriever x Poodle) and the Labradoodle (Labrador Retriever x Poodle).

Sometimes these designer dogs have a practical use for buyers – the Labrador Retriever, for example, sheds less hair than the Poodle and is a good choice for people allergic to dog fur. However the mini designer dogs (which are made by crossing small breeds like Pomeranians, Chihuahuas, Yorkshire Terriers and Poodles) merely serve as adorable lap dogs.

MIXED BREED

There are millions of dogs in the world whose ancestry is unknown, and these are often called mongrels. Since all breeds of dogs can interbreed, they can have genes from just about everywhere. Some people are not snobbish about having mixed-breed dogs as family pets, but sadly, many are. So many mixed-breed dogs in perfect health end up in rescue shelters.

All over the world, mixed breed dogs have nicknames ranging from the derogatory to the funny.

- In the UK, a mixed breed is called a mongrel, cur, tyke or mutt.

- In the Bahamas, they are called 'potcakes' – a reference to the leftovers at the bottom of the pot that are fed to dogs.

- In the Dominican Republic and Brazil, they are called 'trash can tippers' because they often knock over rubbish bins to reach the refuse that they feed on.

- In Newfoundland, a small mixed-breed dog is called a 'cracky'.

Breed *v.* lifespan

A dog's lifespan has a lot to do with the size of its breed. As a general rule, a dog of a smaller breed will live longer than a dog of a larger breed.

- *A large-breed dog is elderly by the age of five.*
- *A medium-sized breed is elderly by seven.*
- *A small breed doesn't reach old age until 10.*

So, for example, the miniature Chihuahua lives for as long as 15 years, while the whopping Great Dane lives for a mere seven to 10 years.

HOW A BREED IS RECOGNISED

Breeds are registered with the Kennel Club in the UK and there's an interesting history to origins of this procedure:

Dog shows became fashionable in the middle of the 19th century in England. At that time almost all dogs were called Spot or Rover, and it was difficult to identify a particular dog at a show. A system of registration came into place, so that every dog was registered according to its breed (ie its physical characteristics) rather than simply by the name given to it by its owner. Slowly, the system was developed to record the details of every dog and official breed standards were established.

Once a breed is established, it's eligible for registration with the Kennel Club. Before recognition is granted, however, there's a procedure to verify the history, the physical characteristics and the temperament of the breed.

BREEDING CATEGORIES AND STANDARDS

Recently, there has been some debate about whether strict breeding categories are cruel to dogs.

Only purebred dogs are eligible to compete in established dog shows like Crufts, and they have to conform to certain 'breed standards' fixed by the Kennel Club. These breed standards can be bad for the dog's health.

In the elite world of Crufts, as a result of the strict breeding standards, some King Charles Spaniels have brains too large for their skulls, some Boxers are epileptic, some Pugs can't breathe properly and some Bulldogs have difficulty having puppies.

The tiny designer dogs which are in vogue are also not healthy. They've got organs too big to fit into their bodies, or they've got so many teeth they can't eat properly. Like fashion models and gymnasts, the females have reproductive issues and they can only give birth by caesarean section.

Such defects are passed down through genes, because breeders mate dogs who are very closely related in order to preserve breed standards. Sisters are mated with brothers, and mothers mated with sons . . . yes, incest is normal in the world of pedigree dogs!

The debate rages on as to whether this type of obsessive pursuit of the perfect breed standard is worth the manipulation of the animals.

Crufts

Crufts is the largest dog show in the world, held by the Kennel Club in March every year at the NEC, Birmingham. There are prizes for each dog which is deemed to be the best in its breed and its group and the top dog wins 'Best in Show'. There are also lots of prizes for agility, obedience and so on.

The name Crufts comes from the show's 19th century founder, Charles Cruft, who was a corporate bigwig at a dog biscuit company. His observation of dog shows convinced him that there was a need to raise standards. His first dog show was held in 1886 and called the 'First Great Terrier Show,' with 600 entries. Soon afterwards, 'Cruft's Greatest Dog Show' was held in Islington in 1891. It was the first show to let all breeds compete, and there were about 2,500 entries.

The show continued annually, going from strength to strength, until Cruft passed away in 1938. His widow took over for four years, and then sold the event to the Kennel Club. The show has continued since, with 28,000 dogs competing every year and 160,000 people cheering them on.

Until recently only purebred dogs were eligible for dog shows. So while the Kennel Club organises the prestigious 'Crufts' for purebreds, it also holds an alternative show called 'Scrufts' which is open only to crossbreeds and mixed breeds. Pedigrees aren't eligible to compete at this event.

🐕 THE MOST POPULAR 🐕 BREEDS IN THE UK

1. Labrador Retriever
2. Cocker Spaniel
3. English Springer Spaniel
4. German Shepherd Dog (Alsatian)

5. Staffordshire Bull Terrier
6. Cavalier King Charles Spaniel
7. Golden Retriever
8. West Highland White Terrier
9. Boxer
10. Border Terrier
11. Rottweiler
12. Shih Tzu
13. Miniature Schnauzer
14. Lhasa Apso
15. Yorkshire Terrier
16. Bulldog
17. Doberman
18. Bull Terrier
19. Weimaraner
20. Pug

Source: The Kennel Club

🐕 CHARACTERISTICS OF MOST 🐕 POPULAR BREEDS

BICHON FRISÉ

Size: small to medium
Training: relatively easy
As a watchdog: too friendly to scare off intruders
Life expectancy: 12–15 years

• Often compared to a cotton ball or a powder puff, because it has a double coat with curls of white, and shades of cream, buff or apricot.

- Standing 24cm–28cm high, quite a bit of grooming is required to maintain its hairstyle, but it doesn't shed much, which makes it a good choice for allergy sufferers.

- Temperament-wise, lives happily in a family with young children.

- Historically, its playful nature made it a good companion dog for 13th century Spanish sailors and for the French royal court. Its looks and nature also suited it to the role of circus dog.

BORDER TERRIER

Size: small to medium
Training: relatively easy but can get distracted
As a watchdog: can be aggressive to unfamiliar faces
Life expectancy: 12–15 years

- Border Terriers have triangle shaped ears which drop forwards on the sides of their heads and are distinguishable by their otter shaped head. They have short tails and a narrow body.

- Originally bred to hunt foxes and other vermin, the Border Terrier can have lots of energy. They need plenty of exercise.

- They can live happily with other animals if they are socialised at a young age. They will still chase unfamiliar animals which they consider to be vermin though; be it a mouse or your pet cat.

- Affectionate so good with children.

- Intelligent breed but they can be stubborn. They also have a very high tolerance for pain so owners should watch carefully for any signs of illness or injury.

BOXER

Size: medium to large
Training: relatively easy
As a watchdog: good
Life expectancy: 10–12 years

- Boxers have a strong medium build, with evident muscles and strength. They have large cheeks and their short hair is generally a fawn or brondle colour, sometimes with white markings.

- Highly energetic so require lots of attention and exercise to prevent boredom and destructive behaviour.

- Fiercely loyal and lovable pet which tends to be good with children, as well as younger animals.

- Were used frequently as circus dogs due to their ability to learn tricks.

- The name 'Boxer' may come from the fact that this dog likes to use its front paws for many tasks.

BULLDOG

Also known as: British Bulldog, English Bulldog
Size: medium
Training: intelligent but can be lazy and slow to train
As a watchdog: good
Life expectancy: 8–10 years

- Well-known for their characteristic face and stocky build.

- Originally bred for the sport of bull-baiting but they are well regarded for their affectionate, if lazy, nature.

- Good with children and make good family pets.

- Known to snore loudly as a result of their restricted airway.

BULL TERRIER

Size: small to medium
Training: difficult
As a watchdog: excellent
Life expectancy: 10–12 years

- The Bull Terrier's most striking features are its long, egg shaped head and deep set triangular eyes. They are small and muscular and generally have dark eyes.

- Originally bred as a companion dog, by crossing a Bulldog with a terrier, they can sometimes be confused with a Pit Bull Terrier.

- Strong, powerful dog which can be difficult to train. Not ideal for a first-time owner.

- Affectionate pets and can be very defensive of owners, especially children. Sometimes referred to as the 'nanny dog'.

- Can be aggressive towards other dogs.

- Intelligent and active breed which requires a lot of exercise.

CAVALIER KING CHARLES SPANIEL

Size: small
Training: relatively easy
As a watchdog: too friendly to make a good watchdog
Life expectancy: 10–14 years

- This Spaniel is a small dog with a silky coat and long ears and large round eyes.

- Originally bred as a lap dog, they are highly affectionate pets.

- Highly sociable so good with other animals. This does mean they can't be left on their own for long periods of time.

- Intelligent breed and quick learners.

- Name comes from Stuart times when they were granted their royal title and Charles II was reportedly never without his pet Spaniels.

- Can gain weight easily.

CHIHUAHUA

Size: very small
Training: not that hard
As a watchdog: yaps, but its sheer lack of size doesn't help
Life expectancy: 15 years

- Big head with foxy ears is disproportionate to its tiny body (23cm high and 1.5kg in weight, on average).

- Despite its puny build, is actually quite tough and loves its owner enough to attack if it senses something is wrong.

- Needs early training to become a sociable being, as it can be insecure with other people or animals.

- A warm-weather dog which comes from a Mexican state that gave the dog its name.

COCKER SPANIEL

Size: small
Training: easy
As a watchdog: will bark at strangers
Life expectancy: 10–14 years

- The large, expressive eyes are endearing, as are its long, floppy ears.

- Stands about 35cm–40cm tall and has a very strokeable silky coat.

- In colour, the coat ranges from soft pastel browns to ebony black.

- Slightly smaller than the English Springer Spaniel, and its coat is coloured from white to white with red and blue marking.

- Playful by nature and the life and soul of the party when it comes to the company of children, other animals and even strangers.

- Eager to please, so it's easy to train them, and they make a good fit for the veteran dog-owner as well as the greenhorn.

COLLIE

Also known as: including Border Collie and Bearded Collie
Size: medium to large
Training: depends on the Collie involved, but generally not bad
As a watchdog: reasonably good, and will bark at strangers
Life expectancy: 10–14 years

- They range from 55cm to 66cm in height.

- Generally, this dog has a pointed snout and erect, foxy ears, like the TV star Lassie, but this profile will differ depending on the Collie type: the Border Collie in Britain, the Rough Collie in the US, or the Bearded Collie.

- The colour of the substantial coat can vary from white and black to sable and even blue.

- They love outdoors activities with the family, especially with children.

- The Collie was bred to be a herding dog in Scotland.

DALMATIAN

Size: medium to large
Training: relatively easy
As a watchdog: reasonably good
Life expectancy: 12–14 years

- Thanks to the movie *101 Dalmatians*, nearly everyone knows this dog with its characteristic elegant carriage and its white coat with black spots.

- Lots of energy to run and lots of willpower to have its own way in everything.

- Needs training to make it a sociable creature, especially with children.

- It originally served as a guard dog for palaces in Croatia. After it was brought to England in 1862, it ran alongside horse-drawn coaches (even now, Dalmatians quite like the company of horses).

DOBERMAN

Also known as: Doberman Pinscher, Dobermann
Size: large
Training: relatively easy
As a watchdog: excellent, originally bred to be guard dogs
Life expectancy: 10–14 years

- Said to have been bred by a German tax collector (named Doberman) as his personal protection dog.

- Often used as police dogs and was also used during the war for guard and messenger duties.

- Dobermans are highly intelligent and can be easily trained.

ENGLISH SPRINGER SPANIEL

Size: medium
Training: easy
As a watchdog: too friendly, but will bark sporadically
Life expectancy: 12–14 years

- Gun Dog, bred to flush out woodcocks from dense undergrowth during hunting.

- Recognisable by its long ears, big brown eyes and alert, trusting expression.

- The coat is either black-and-white, liver-and-white, or a combination of this with tan markings (usually on the cheeks and above the eyes).

- Makes an excellent family dog, due to its easygoing and intelligent nature.

- It is very active, and needs plenty of stimulation and activity.

- It is the fastest of the Spaniels, because of its longer legs.

GERMAN SHEPHERD

Also known as: Alsatian, Deutscher Schaeferhund
Size: large
Training: easy
As a watchdog: very good, barks and may even attack
Life expectancy: 12–14 years

- With its keen, intelligent eyes and dignified mien it looks like a bearded intellectual or a military officer, depending on its individual personality.

- Its height can range from 55cm–65cm, and it has a hard coat in vivid black, tan or sable.

- It can make for a loyal and protective companion, and with children there is no better babysitter. But it needs to be raised with young children to take to them, and it may be aloof when with strangers, or aggressive towards other dogs.

- For these qualities the German Shepherd is frequently employed as a police dog or search-and-rescue dog. Such work is a modern manifestation of its earlier role as a shepherd in Germany.

GOLDEN RETRIEVER

Also known as: Yellow Retriever
Size: large
As a watchdog: pathetic – too refined to bark at strangers
Training: easy
Life expectancy: 10–14 years

- Standing 50cm–60cm tall, the Golden Retriever has a soft, flat or wavy coat in a shade of cream, sand or amaretto.

- The perfect nanny to young children, it gets along famously with other pets and strangers and is popular as a guide dog for the same reason.

- Keep an eye on your furniture, because it's a dog that loves to chew.

- This dog is a swimming champion, a quality that served it well when it used to work as a water Retriever on hunts.

GREAT DANE

Also known as: Danish Hound, Boarhound or German Mastiff
Size: very large
Training: relatively easy but must begin from an early age. Owner must be able to have dominance due to size and strength

As a watchdog: good, very loud bark and strong attachment to owners. Not generally aggressive
Life expectancy: 7–10 years

- One of the largest dog breeds in the world, it currently holds the record for the world's tallest dog.

- These gentle giants are known for their great affection.

- Due to their size this can be an expensive dog to own; at just eight weeks a Great Dane puppy has already grown by 30lbs.

- They need a lot of exercise but are great with children and make very loving pets.

JACK RUSSELL TERRIER

Size: small
Training: relatively easy
As a watchdog: reasonable, will bark
Life expectancy: 13–15 years

- A dog of small size and tough build, standing 30cm–35cm tall.

- With a short coat coloured in white with tan or black markings, its ears fly at half-mast.

- This dog is a good fit for anyone who wants an active play companion, so is perfect for a family with young children because its nature will keep the young ones in tow.

- That behaviour is a tamed form of its former role as a hunting dog in fox-hunts.

- The dog's name comes from the 19th century figure Reverend John Russell, whose terriers followed his hounds and flushed out the foxes from their dens.

LABRADOR RETRIEVER

Also known as: Labrador, Lab
Size: large
Training: easy
As a watchdog: not so good
Life expectancy: 12–13 years

- This large dog with its gentle expression comes in black, chocolate, russet and cream, developed over its dense coat and a height ranging from 55cm to 65cm.

- Here is your perfect family pet, consistently topping the top 10 list in the UK as well as other countries. That's because it will play ball patiently for hours with a tireless child, or lie quietly without getting in the way.

- It's physically well-equipped to give strangers such a welcome that it can knock them over in the urge to say hello, so you need to take care of that with early training.

- Well-mannered Labradors are used for therapy at hospitals, guide dogs for the blind, and their keen sense of smell makes them good as sniffer dogs at the airport.

- Its stable temperament and physical strength made it a good fisherman's companion in Newfoundland, where it retrieved fishing nets before it was imported to England.

LHASA APSO

Size: small
Training: relatively easy
As a watchdog: good
Life expectancy: 15–18 years

- Lhasa Apso's have a long coat which is very dense, in fact the name means 'long-haired Tibetan dog'.

- Originally bred as a watchdog in Buddhist monasteries in Tibet, to warn the monks of any intruders.

- Have a very loud bark despite their size.

- Intelligent dogs which are loyal to their family but can be mistrustful of strangers.

- Require early socialisation and training but are eager to please their owner.

- Their long hair requires regular bathing and grooming.

MINIATURE SCHNAUZER

Size: small
Training: easy
As a watchdog: good
Life expectancy: 12–15 years

- The miniature Schnauzer has 'V' shaped ears which droop forward as well as a discernable chin and moustache whiskers.

- This breed was developed as a farm dog to hunt rats by crossing Schnauzers with smaller breeds such as Poodles.

- Can bark a lot but will be loyal and not over-aggressive to strangers.

- Highly energetic but they are intelligent and easy to train.

- They are good with children and other animals if socialised from an early age. They will follow their hunting instincts and chase small animals.

PUG

Size: small
Training: relatively easy
As a watchdog: not great
Life expectancy: 12–15 years

- Pugs are recognisable by their wrinkly face and have a friendly demeanour despite their stern expression.

- Require a lot of attention and often stay with their owner at all times. They are sociable but can be stubborn.

- Pugs were bred to be lap dogs during the Shang dynasty in China.

- Pugs have a tendency to snore due to their flat face shape.

- They prefer the company of people to other dogs.

ROTTWEILER

Size: large
Training: relatively easy (more work needed for family pet)
As a watchdog: excellent
Life expectancy: 9–10 years

- Height ranges from 55cm to 70cm, and it has a lithe black coat with tan markings.

- They need a lot of training to make them family pets. The Rottweiler can get seriously annoyed by an inquisitive toddler, so make sure it stays emperor of not only its own bed but its own playground as well.

- This dog's fierce and courageous nature makes it a good police dog or guard dog.

SETTER

Size: medium to large
Training: relatively easy
As a watchdog: effective
Life expectancy: 10–12 years

- The sweet-natured Setter boasts cascades of ears on either side of its head, and a straight, silky coat, usually white, with flecks in blue, orange or liver for the English Setter, and Golden or a rich chestnut for the Irish Setter. The hair can extend all the way to in between the Setter's toes.

- Its height ranges from 55cm to 65cm and can therefore be slightly overwhelming if you have young children.

- Setters share their gregarious nature with Spaniels, from whom they were bred in Spain and exported to Britain and France.

SHIH TZU

Also known as: 'Lion Dog' in Chinese, Xi Shi Quan or the Chrysanthemum dog
Size: small
Training: can be difficult
As a watchdog: good, feisty temperament but disadvantaged by its size
Life expectancy: 10–18 years

- Known for their long silky coat which needs to be brushed daily.

- Believed to have been kept as pets in the Chinese palace court.

- Friendly but can have an obstinate streak, which some believe results from their aristocratic origins.

STAFFORDSHIRE BULL TERRIER

Size: medium
Training: relatively easy but needs firm handling
As a watchdog: good
Life expectancy: 12–14 years

- The Staffordshire bull terrier has a strong stocky build with short ears and pronounced cheek muscles.

- Originally bred for bull baiting, this English breed is related to other bull terrier breeds, which are all categorised as Pit Bull Terriers.

- Brave and tenacious breed which can seem intimidating but in fact make great family pets with the proper training.

- Nicknamed 'staffies' this breed has received bad press, but it's distinguished in the UK from the American Bull Terrier which is subject to breed legislation.

- Need regular exercise and proper socialisation to prevent them becoming aggressive.

WEIMARANER

Size: medium to large
Training: relatively easy
As a watchdog: good
Life expectancy: 10–12 years

- The Weimaraner has an athletic build, which many describe as noble. Their grey colour is their most discernable feature.

- The grey coat colour of this breed is a result of a recessive gene and has led to the nickname 'the grey ghost'.

- Originally bred as royal hunting dogs to hunt large prey such as boars and deer.

- Territorial and protective of their family, the Weimaraner is not always as friendly as other hunting dogs.

- Highly intelligent dogs which need a lot of exercise.

WEST HIGHLAND WHITE TERRIER

Size: small
Training: relatively easy with a firm hand
As a watchdog: good
Life expectancy: 9–15 years

- These terriers have bright, deep set eyes, pointy ears and a carrot shaped tail. They are mostly recognised by their white coat.

- Nicknamed 'westies', this breed originated in Scotland where it was bred to hunt foxes and badgers.

- Small but stocky breed which is friendly and inquisitive.

- Active dogs which need a lot of exercise.

- Good companions and good with children but must know who's in charge to stop them becoming naughty.

YORKSHIRE TERRIER

Also known as: Yorkie, Broken-haired Scotch Terrier
Size: small
Training: relatively easy
As a watchdog: will definitely bark but its size and the toy looks don't help
Life expectancy: 12–15 years

- One of the world's smallest breeds, standing at only 18cm–20cm.

- It has dark, beady eyes and its ears stand erect. It has a coat of long, silky, glossy hair that is black and tan.

- A Yorkie is a precious being: a careless child could crush it, and it needs a jumper in cold or wet weather.

- Yorkies get along fine with children and people generally, as well as other pets. If the pets happen to be bigger dogs there may be a problem, because the Yorkie has a strong territorial instinct and will try to show who is boss.

- It needs a safe place to play inside the house as its curious nature may otherwise lead it to bolt through an open door.

🐕 GROUPING OF BREEDS 🐕

People generally refer to dogs either by their breed or their type. Although it may seem that these two terms are interchangeable there is in fact a stark distinction:

- 'Breed' refers to the established pedigree and lineage of a dog: a set of genetic characteristics recognised by the Kennel Club.

- 'Type' refers to a more general category of dog, based on their function or use.

It is important to bear in mind then that when referring to dogs by their type, the dogs within that type may not be physically similar. It merely means they perform similar tasks (or were originally bred to). Thus, while there are more than 200 breeds of dog, there are seven groups recognised by the Kennel Club in the UK.

The main dog groups are:

1. Working

2. Pastoral

3. Terrier

4. Hound

5. Gundog

6. Toy

7. Utility

WORKING DOGS

This group can include:

- St Bernard
- Siberian Husky
- Rottweiler
- Boxer
- Doberman
- Great Dane
- Newfoundland
- Portuguese Water Dog

This group of dogs were originally bred to be rescue or guard dogs and of course many dogs still perform these valuable services today. Among other things, search-and-rescue dogs find injured people trapped in earthquake debris, and police dogs aid the police force in sniffing out drugs. Working dogs are usually large, though some, like those for hearing-impaired people, may be small enough to be carried in the lap.

Working dogs by nature are highly intelligent and therefore make excellent pets if they are given enough stimulation and exercise. They respond well to training and thrive in competitions.

PASTORAL DOGS

This group can include:

- Bearded Collie
- Border Collie

- Collie

- Alsatian (German Shepherd)

- Old English Sheepdog

- Welsh Corgi

The pastoral group's main purpose is that of herding sheep or cattle, or sometimes other animals, or to guard livestock. The dogs have a variety of techniques when it comes to their herding duties:

- When the Border Collie has to make its target animal move, it will get in front of it and give it the 'strong eye'. This is called a 'header'.

- Other dogs, like the Australian Cattle Dog, make the target animal move by nipping at its heels. This is called a 'heeler'.

- And then there are the dogs who will get the job done, by header or by heeler, or even by jumping on the animal's back.

Pocket fact 🐾

As pastoral breeds have to work the year round, come rain or shine, it helps that they have a double waterproof coat.

Pastoral breeds make great family pets thanks to their temper and intelligence. But they're more suitable for active and sporty people than for stay-at-homes types. Unless you keep them doing something interesting, they will start herding or harassing hapless runners or bikers on the street. It's just another form of the modified predatory behaviour they exhibit when they herd sheep.

TERRIERS

This group, as the name suggests, is made up of the terrier breeds and can include:

- Airedale Terrier

- Border Terrier

- Bull Terrier

- Fox Terrier

- Irish Terrier

- Welsh Terrier

- West Highland White Terrier

This group were originally bred to hunt vermin, and the name terrier comes from the word 'terra' which means 'earth'; terriers just love to dig!

With their burrowing habits and penchant for catching mice and rabbits, terriers were bred to be hardy and brave, often chasing larger animals such as badgers underground. They could also scare off foxes marauding chicken coops.

They are a diverse group physically, but they are all well equipped for their roles. They are small enough to squeeze into holes and to nip into crannies. They have tough coats which can stand up to thorny bushes and bad weather.

Terriers can make cute family pets, but you need to make sure they don't run away thanks to their instinctive digging habits. Set up a fence buried in the earth, and give them some toys to distract them from the plant life in your garden. Also, be extra careful when introducing a terrier to a cat. And no matter how tame a terrier appears, a guinea pig or a rabbit is liable to set its predatory instincts going.

A much-maligned dog: the Pit Bull Terrier

The term 'Pit Bull' encompasses a number of breeds developed from terrier and bulldog crosses in 19th century England. They include the Bull Terrier, the American Pit Bull Terrier, and the Staffordshire Pit Bull Terrier. Mongrels that are not easy to classify will fall into the Pit Bull classification if they have a substantial number of the physical characteristics of a Pit Bull Terrier.

The Pit Bull breed was originally developed for bull baiting or to fight other dogs. Unfortunately, illegal dog fighting continues, as unscrupulous breeders mistreat Pit Bulls in order to make them aggressive.

The Pit Bull Terrier has been ill-reputed in recent times because of attacks on humans, notably young children. In 1991 the Dangerous Dog Act was passed, in which it states that Pit Bulls must be muzzled and kept on a leash in public. They must also be registered and insured, neutered, tattooed and receive microchip implants. The Act also bans the breeding, sale and exchange of the Pit Bull Terrier breeds, excluding the Staffordshire Pit Bull Terrier.

Under the act it is illegal to own any of the other Pit Bull Terrier breeds and the police can get a warrant to seize the dog. Any dog seized cannot be put down without the consent of the owner. If the owner does not give consent then legal proceedings begin. Although it is still legal to own a Staffordshire Pit Bull Terrier there is some debate over whether Irish Staffordshire Bull Terriers fall under this same legal protection and owners can face the same legal proceedings as other Pit Bull breed owners. Contact the Kennel Club for more details on the legal restrictions on owning a Pit Bull Terrier.

HOUNDS

This group can include:

- Afghan Hound
- Basset Hound
- Beagle
- Bloodhound

- Dachshund

- Deerhound

- Greyhound

- Irish Wolfhound

- Whippet

> *Pocket fact* 🐾
>
> *The Greyhound is the fastest dog in the world. It can sprint at speeds of 70km per hour.*

When we talk about 'hounding someone to death' today, that's because it's exactly what hounds were trained to do, and was the main purpose for the development of this group. Hounds would either follow up their prey through sight (like the Greyhound) or through scent (like the Bloodhound).

> *Pocket fact* 🐾
>
> *It's said that the Greyhound, Bloodhound and Mastiff owe their origins (as breeds) to the ancient Greeks and Romans.*

Hounds come in all shapes and sizes. The Basset Hound is short and the Irish Wolfhound is one of the tallest dogs. Hounds also have a great variety of coats. The Afghan Hound or Saluki, is practically robed by its hair, while the Beagle has very short hair. The different ways in which hounds would track their prey also add great variety to this group:

- Scent hounds were selectively bred for sniffing out quarry. Scent hounds include Bassets, Beagles, Bloodhounds, Dachshunds, Foxhounds, Norwegian Elkhounds, Otterhounds etc.

Pocket fact ❀

Since fox-hunting was made illegal in the UK in 2005, hounds can be used to follow up a scent but aren't allowed to kill foxes.

- Sight hounds have been employed to track game by their sight. Sight hounds include Greyhounds, Whippets, Afghan Hounds, Russian Wolfhounds, Ibizan Hounds, Irish Wolfhounds, Pharaoh Hounds, Rhodesian Ridgebacks, and Scottish Deerhounds.

- Greyhounds have a history going back to the ancient times of the Egyptian Pharaohs, when they were painted on the walls of tombs. Greyhounds come in many colours, not just grey, and many Greyhounds which are family pets today are mostly older dogs, retired from the racetracks.

Greyhound racing

Greyhound racing as an organised sport began in Emeryville, California, in 1919. The sport came to England in 1926, and today Greyhound races are a feature of British rather than American culture.

In the race, the Greyhounds pursue a mechanical 'hare' around the track. This is because the sport of racing developed from the older sport of 'coursing' where Greyhounds had to pursue hares, rabbits and foxes in aristocratic hunts. Coursing an actual hare is forbidden by law in many countries including the UK, but the practice exists as the sport of 'lure coursing' where two Greyhounds compete against each other to chase a 'lure' of a white plastic bag.

Greyhound racing is a money-making business: the dogs are track stars and huge bets are placed on every dog. Greyhounds are raced until the age of four at the most, and then retire.

Retirement for some means switching to the life of a family pet, or being given up to a rescue home in the hope of finding a home (the Retired Greyhound Trust is the most well-known of these organisations). But fate is less kind to other Greyhounds, who may be drowned or shot, or exported to countries with warm weather to be raced. Some Greyhounds are abandoned and become homeless.

The hunting origins of this group don't mean that a hound is too savage to be a family pet. Hounds aren't the most extrovert of dogs, and they become very attached to their human family and make great company for children. You should be careful with them around cats though, as they love to chase anything that looks small and weak enough.

GUNDOGS

This group can include:

- English Setter

- Pointer

- Golden Retriever

- Spaniel

Gundogs were bred for the hunt. Their role was to find the game, flush it out and fetch it for the owner once it had been shot down. But their history of predatory roles doesn't mean they don't make great pets – in fact, they make the friendliest family companions, and are ideal for households with children. They are clever and busy dogs, and they expect the same of you.

Gundogs come in all sizes, ranging from the Labrador Retriever to the Cocker Spaniel. The standard Poodle is also classed as a gundog while the Toy and Miniature Poodle are placed in the toy group. The coats of gundogs protect them when they plunge through shrubbery, so they can be a handful to brush.

There are three kinds of gundogs, based on their roles while hunting:

- Setters search the target (usually birds) and 'set' or freeze when they find it. Examples include the English Setter and the Irish Setter.

- Pointers flush out the birds that the owner can then shoot. Examples include the German Short-haired Pointer, Hungarian Vizla and Spaniels.

- Retrievers retrieve the game. Examples are the Labrador Retriever and the Golden Retriever.

Hair-raising swim

Today, people love the Poodle for its distinctive coiffure, including its shaped pom-poms. But a poodle's 'hairstyle' used to be more than an ornamental tuft, given its original purpose as a water Retriever. The heavy coat was clipped so as to make the dog more efficient in the water, and the pom-poms kept its joints warm. The Poodle has also been used to find and retrieve truffles in the forest.

The Poodle is thought to have come from Germany. But it was adored by the French, who bred the Poodle into its current form; it even became the national dog of France.

TOY DOGS

This group can include:

- Bichon Frisé
- Cavalier King Charles Spaniel
- Chihuahua
- Maltese
- Pekingese
- Pug
- Pomeranian
- Yorkshire Terrier
- Poodle (Miniature or Toy)

Toy dogs were just that – breeds which were meant as toys for those who could afford them.

Pocket fact ❧
The smallest dog is the Chihuahua, at 25cm long and weighing just 2kg.

These dogs weren't meant to work in the first place, but to look nice and to be companions for noble ladies in the dog-eat-dog atmosphere of royal courts. Their diminutive size enabled them to be lovingly placed on a lady's lap, hence the term 'lap dog'. They served as status symbols too – a tradition which continues today.

Today, toy dogs aren't confined to the wealthy. But they continue their role as companions, especially to the elderly as they require little exercise but need many hours of loving attention. They retain their lordly habits in their eating habits sometimes, being gourmets in their tastes.

Their coats need regular brushing, but a Cavalier King Charles Spaniel is a good choice for those whose hands and time won't permit long hours of grooming.

A dog for tea?

Sometimes breeders make extra-cute versions of toy dogs, which are called 'teacup dogs'. This is not a technical term, and is not recognised as such by the Kennel Club. It simply describes a dog which is usually smaller than its breed standard.

Critics of the term dismiss it as a clever marketing ploy. Yorkshire Terriers, Chihuahuas, and miniature Pinschers can all be described as teacup dogs.

Though teacup pooches look cute, they might have long-term health problems because their organs are all crowded into a small body. See p.14 for the downsides of a dog that's chiefly bred for its looks.

UTILITY DOGS

This group can include:

- Akita

- Boston Terrier

- Bulldog

- Dalmatian

- Standard Poodle

- Shar Pei

- Shih Tzu

This is a somewhat miscellaneous group of breeds which have not been bred for one specific purpose but are useful for a purpose not covered by the working or sporting categories.

Some of the dogs in this group were originally bred for a purpose which is now extinct, such as the Bulldog, which was used for bull baiting, or the Lhasa Apso, which served as a temple dog in Tibet.

As there is such a range of breeds within this group it is best to research each individual breed when deciding whether that type of dog would make a suitable pet for your family.

Here are a few other dog groups which you may have heard of, but which are not officially termed as groups:

SLED DOGS

Sled dogs, including the Alaskan Huskies, are used in Arctic climes to pull sleds. They are a kind of dog rather than an official breed, dating back about 10,000 years and derived from Siberian Huskies.

Sled dogs can be purebreds like Siberian Huskies, Samoyeds, Eskimo dogs, Alaskan Malamutes and so on. These are all large, strong, bad-weather dogs with thick coats.

They were used to pull sleds and were employed by Eskimos for transport, and later in Alaska for freight and mail delivery, as well as by fur-trappers for travelling. Today, although snowmobiles and airlines do most of the transport, some sled dogs still share a bit of the responsibility. But most sled dogs nowadays serve for recreation at the races. It's a big sport in Alaska, Canada and Norway.

'Fashionable' dogs

Sales of different breeds are a curious phenomenon, and often go up and down with what people see in the movies and in the media.

The film Babe helped many Border Collie puppies find homes. This turned out to be a case of choose in haste, repent at leisure for some though. Border Collies are farm dogs and a very agile breed, and they always need to be kept busy. Most owners hadn't taken this into the equation, as a result of which many adult Border Collies ended up in rescue homes.

When the film 101 Dalmatians came out in 1996, sales of Dalmatians soared – which later had its flip side, like the sudden popularity of Border Collies. The Dalmatian needs long sprints and lots of exercise to keep it fit. These athletic habits have to be nurtured by a responsible Dalmatian owner.

The breeds of dogs which are currently experiencing a popularity surge are:

- *Portuguese Water Dog (thanks to President Obama)*
- *Chihuahua*
- *Designer breeds such as labradoodles and puggles*

However, the Labrador Retriever continues to be the most popular breed of dog in both the UK and the US, topping the list of the number of Kennel Club registrations in 2006, 2007 and 2008.

Dog sledding races

Alaskan Huskies are the dogs mostly featured in these races. Alaskan Huskies are physically well-equipped to deal with these trials of endurance, with their thick, fluffy coats.

Sled dogs usually race in teams. A dog team is guided by the human trainer, called a 'musher'. The team is guided by the musher's voice commands, like 'Gee' (turn right), and 'Haw' (turn left). The voice commands are picked up by a lead dog, also called a command leader.

The cross-country races vary in length. They can be sprints of around 50km, mid-distance races of 80km–320km, or long-distance races of 320km–1,600km. Teams usually consist of four to 10 dogs. A six to eight-dog team can pull a sled at a speed of more than 30km per hour.

🐕 WILD DOGS 🐕

Although dogs are descended from wolves and many dogs are now domesticated, there are still wild dogs to be found in the world.

DINGO

- This Australian wild dog is sometimes known by its nickname 'the singing dog' and is also found in Malaysia, Thailand, the Philippines and New Guinea. The dingo gets its nickname because of its impressive vocal range of howls. It doesn't bark that often.

- It's thought that the dingo was brought in from Asia by sea travellers, since the first dingo fossil in Australia is around 3,500 years old.

- Dingos typically live in packs like wolves, and they howl to show that they've asserted themselves in a territory.

- They used to prey on marsupials like kangaroos and wallabies, but changed their diet when the European rabbit was introduced in the 19th century.

- Dingos are regarded as pests in many farming areas as they sometimes prey on livestock.

- The Dingo breed is being diluted today through interbreeding with domestic dogs, as human settlements continue to spread and impinge on their territory.

AFRICAN HUNTING DOG

- The African Hunting Dog is renowned for having the stripes of a tiger and the spots of a leopard all rolled into a canine being. Its irregular yet sleek anatomy hints at the confusion surrounding its name – it's also called the African Wild Dog and the Cape Hunting Dog, as well as the 'spotted dog' and the 'painted wolf'.

- Found in southern Africa and east of the Sahara, this dog retains its ancestral habits by hunting in packs of anything from 15 to 60 dogs.

- These dogs have been known to hunt horned antelopes and sometimes they even go after cattle on the outskirts of human settlements.

BUSH DOG

- This dog could be termed the Chihuahua of the wild, standing all of 30cm high.

- The bush dog lives – just as its name suggests – hidden in the bushes, in rainforest shrubbery or savannah grass. Rarely is the shy bush dog ever seen by the human eye.

- Unfortunately, it's likely that the sight of a bush dog will get even rarer with time, as humans continue to encroach on its natural habitat.

Dogs as food

In countries without a long tradition of keeping dogs as pets, such as parts of East and South-East Asia, dog meat can be a delicacy. When the 2002 FIFA World Cup was held in South Korea, the football was dogged by a food controversy as FIFA called for a ban on eating dog meat.

Brigitte Bardot, the French actress-turned-activist, railed against the 'barbaric' practice. Korean critics hit back at what they perceived as the 'racism' of her statements, pointing out that they didn't understand how snails and horses could happily be eaten in France.

🐕 MAN'S BEST FRIEND: 🐕 DOGS WHO HELP US

POLICE DOGS

Although these dogs aren't made up of one particular group or breed, this is a group of dogs which well deserves the title of man's best friend.

There are records of Bloodhounds being used for police work as early as the 18th century, but the formal training of police dogs began in Belgium and Germany through First World War dogs that were used for guard duty.

In the Second World War, soldiers of the Allied forces brought home reports of what they had observed. Training centres were set up in London and elsewhere throughout Europe, and gradually spread to the rest of the world.

Today, police dogs are key to law enforcement. German Shepherds are commonly used, but the Doberman Pinscher or Labrador Retriever are also used sometimes.

Dogs which don't have the docile temperament to make good family pets are often very useful as police dogs, where the sheer sight of a growling dog can sometimes force a criminal to surrender instead of fleeing. If there's physical confrontation, the dog usually gets the better of it.

9/11 HEROES

More than 300 police dogs helped the victims of the September 11 World Trade Center terror attacks in New York City. Sirius, a bomb detection dog attached to the Port Authority Police Department, lost his life when the towers collapsed.

A police dog's acute sense of hearing is crucial to its work. Since dogs can hear higher frequencies than human beings, they can be called and trained with dog whistles that are silent to the human ear but clearly audible to dogs.

SNIFFER DOGS

Some police dogs are scent-detectives who search for illegal drugs, explosives or fugitives in hiding. However, sniffer dogs aren't used for police work alone – for example, Springer Spaniels have been employed to search out bumblebee nests, for the conservation of endangered species of bees.

The amazing thing about sniffer dogs is that their noses are so sensitive that they can sniff out a scent even when it is masked by other scents. Drug smugglers often try to fool security forces by wrapping drugs in perfumes or spices, but dogs still pick out the drugs. It helps the dogs that they have about 200 million scent-receptor cells in their noses, while the average human has only five million.

GUIDE DOGS

Guide dogs for the visually impaired are a familiar presence in our lives, and it's interesting that dogs, who don't have a very good sense of sight themselves, are so good at becoming a substitute pair of eyes.

The practice of training such guide dogs started in Germany during the First World War to help blinded veterans. Today, guide dogs are trained in many countries in training schools often run by non-profit organisations.

The breeds usually chosen to be guide dogs are Labrador Retrievers and Labrador-Golden Retriever crosses, but Doberman Pinschers and German Shepherds are also used sometimes.

A guide dog is trained to help its 'handler' move around. Guide dogs are often allowed in public places where other dogs may not be allowed. They have to perform a variety of roles that call for confidence, concentration and intelligence.

Guide dogs display an amazing faculty called 'selective disobedience'. This means that they disobey their handler when their judgement tells them that their handler might be in danger if they follow the command. This faculty is very important when crossing the road, for example.

At guide dog training schools, puppies are chosen from parents who are the most intelligent and efficient of their breed in terms of guiding ability. When the puppy is a year old, it is trained intensively for three to four months. Not every puppy leaves the school with a degree, though. About 80% qualify to become fully fledged guide dogs.

A guide dog knows it has to be at work when its harness is fastened. At this time it goes into focus mode, and shouldn't be patted by passing admirers, because that will distract it from helping its handler. When the guide dog's harness is off, however, it becomes an ordinary family pet. And then it will be happy with praise and pats.

2

DOGS IN CULTURE

🐕 IN MYTHOLOGY 🐕

Dogs have a long-standing relationship with man, stretching back through time, so it is understandable that there should be a few famous pooches in mythology.

Argos: in Homer's ancient Greek epic *The Odyssey*, the hound Argos waited for over 20 years for his master Odysseus to come home, when most people thought Odysseus was dead. When Odysseus does come back to his kingdom, disguised as a beggar, Argos knows him straight away. He lets out a whimper of welcome, and dies content.

Cerberus: this dog from Greek and Roman mythology guards the gates of Hell, or the underworld. Cerberus is usually shown with three heads, although some sources show more — even as many as 50. As if that were not enough, it boasts a mane of live snakes and, to top it all, a dragon's tail.

Cerberus may owe his fearful appearance to his infamous parents. His mother is Echidna, a half-woman half-serpent, and his father is Typhon, a terrible giant who breathes fire.

The last of the 12 labours of Hercules, assigned by King Eurystheus, was to capture Cerberus. When Hercules captured the beast the king was so frightened that he immediately ordered Cerberus to be taken back to the underworld again.

The Beddgelert Dog: the Welsh legend of Gelert tells of Llywelyn the Great, Prince of Gwynedd, who returned from a hunting trip and found his baby missing.

His dog Gelert had blood smeared over its mouth. Llywelyn thought that the dog had killed his child, and in turn, killed the dog with his sword. Soon afterwards, Llywelyn heard the baby crying, and found it uninjured under its cradle, along with a dead wolf that Gelert had killed to save the baby. A penitent Llywelyn buried the dead Gelert with due honour.

No-one knows for sure if Gelert really existed, although there is a memorial in the village of Beddgelert. But the story reflects just how loyal a dog can be. It also shows how the fear of a dog attack isn't unique to our times.

Anubis: the Egyptian god of mummification and the underworld, Anubis, is depicted as having the head of a jackal.

> *Pocket fact* 🐾
>
> *The werewolf (a human with the ability to change into a wolf during the full moon) has been a popular figure in mythology since ancient Greece, and even now appears in horror films.*

🐕 IN HISTORY 🐕

- The ceramics of ancient Iran and the tombs of the Pharaohs in Egypt sport pictures of a dog which looks a lot like the modern dog breed Saluki. Dog mummies have often been found with those of Pharaohs in pyramids.

- In 79 AD, after the Roman city Pompeii was destroyed by the volcanic eruption of Mount Vesuvius, a dead dog was found in the debris, spread-eagled over a dead child. It looked as though the dog had lost its life in trying to protect the child.

- There is a bronze statue of a dog called Hachiko in Shibuya station in Tokyo. Hachiko was an Akita dog who belonged to a university professor. Every morning Hachiko would see his master off at the train station, and welcome him back every evening. One day Hachiko's master failed to return – he had died of a stroke. Hachiko went to greet his master at the station that evening, and returned every evening for the next 10 years until the end of his own life.

Pocket fact 🐾

The earliest 'beware of the dog' sign was discovered in a house in ancient Pompeii. The mosaic, found on the floor of the entrance hall, bears the inscription 'cave canem'.

🐕 IN LITERATURE 🐕

The Hound of the Baskervilles (1901–1902): Sir Arthur Conan Doyle's inspiration for the huge killer hound in this novel may have come from the legend of Black Shuck, a ghost dog said to run on the moors in Norfolk.

Cujo (1981): Stephen King's psychological horror novel centres on a family pet called Cujo whose owner forgets to vaccinate him against rabies. While chasing rabbits, Cujo's head gets stuck in a hole. A bite by a rabid bat turns him into the terror of the countryside.

Bullseye in *Oliver Twist:* Charles Dickens' evil Bull Terrier is an alter ego of its mean and vicious owner Bill Sikes. When Sikes murders Nancy, Bullseye leaves bloody paw-prints on the floor, as though he is writing out Sikes' guilty conscience. Gradually, Sikes becomes obsessed and feels he must somehow get rid of the dog, as Bullseye's name keeps conjuring up Nancy's accusing eyes to the haunted Sikes.

Buck, in Jack London's *The Call of the Wild* (1903): Buck is a St. Bernard/Scots Shepherd (a Collie) cross. The novel traces Buck's coming-of-age as he is stolen and forced to become a sled dog in Alaska during the Gold Rush. Gradually, Buck betters himself as he challenges the lead dog Spitz in a fight to the death. Having earned his place, Buck survives many more hardships to become a celebrity sled dog when he pulls a sled weighing a ton from the frozen ice all by himself. When his kind owner gets killed, Buck leaves human civilisation altogether and joins a pack of wolves, eventually haunting the land as a Ghost Dog.

The *Harry Potter* books: **Fang** is Hagrid's faithful companion and appears in all of the Harry Potter books. He is depicted as a total wimp despite being a large Boarhound. In *Harry Potter and the Philosopher's Stone* **Fluffy** is a large three-headed dog who guards the entrance to the chamber which houses the philosopher's stone. This guard dog is clearly based on the mythical Cerberus (see p.51). Sirius Black, Harry's godfather, who is an animagus (a magician who can turn into an animal), also appears as the dog **Padfoot** in the novels.

The Hundred and One Dalmatians: Dodie Smith's novel introduced **Pongo** and **Missis** as the parents of the Dalmatian puppies stolen by Cruella De Vil to make a fur coat. The novel is the inspiration for the two Disney film versions.

The Twa Dogs, by Robert Burns: this poem features in Burns' *Kilmarnock Volume* and has two central characters, **Ceasar**, a laird's dog, and **Luath**, a farmer's Collie who discuss the class differences which exist between their two owners. The poem includes the line 'Rejoiced they were not men, but dogs'.

Nana in *Peter Pan:* Nana is a Newfoundland dog and nanny to the Darling children in JM Barrie's play and novel. She is said to be based on Barrie's own dog, a St Bernard called Porthos.

Timmy in *The Famous Five* books: Timmy the dog was a mongrel who made up the fifth member of the Famous Five in Enid Blyton's classic books.

Spot: the star of a series of children's books from the 1980s which were later made into a BBC television series. The pop-up books have been credited as having a huge influence on encouraging young children to read.

Celebrities and their dogs

- *Oprah Winfrey has five dogs including a Cocker Spaniel named Sadie.*
- *Martha Stewart has two French Bulldogs named Francesca and Sharkey.*
- *Rick Stein had a Jack Russell Terrier, Chalky, who had a Sharp's Ale named after him following his death in 2007.*
- *Audrey Hepburn had a Yorkshire Terrier called Mr Famous.*
- *Paris Hilton has a Chihuahua named Tinkerbell.*
- *Frank Sinatra and Dean Martin both owned Greyhounds.*
- *Britney Spears has a Chihuahua named Bit Bit and a Yorkshire Terrier called London.*
- *Justin Timberlake has two Yorkshire Terriers.*
- *Russian President Vladimir Putin has Koni, a Labrador Retriever.*
- *The Queen has several Welsh Corgis.*
- *Sigmund Freud had a Chow Chow which sat in on therapy sessions.*

🐕 IN FILMS 🐕

Dogs have frequently appeared on the silver screen, most often as a loyal companion or as the star of a children's film. Here are some of the canine stars of the cinema.

Lassie: the heroic Collie has a long lineage, going back all the way to a short story called *Lassie Come Home* (1938), by Eric Knight,. A film was made in 1943 with a talented Collie actor called Pal, who shared stardom with Elizabeth Taylor. Pal then appeared in six other Lassie films through the years until 1951. Through 1945–1949, Lassie had her own radio show and the *Lassie* TV series ran for 19 years from 1954. Pal's descendants have made a family tradition of acting the part of Lassie through eight generations. Although Lassie herself is female, the character has been played by male dogs as their coats are thicker and so more photogenic for screen appearances.

Toto: the little black dog from *The Wizard of Oz*. In the evergreen 1939 movie starring Judy Garland, the part of Toto went to a female Cairn Terrier called Terry, who acted in 13 movies. As a film starlet, when she played Toto in the *Wizard of Oz*, she earned more than many of the human actors. The actors who played the diminutive Munchkin people earned only $50 per week, while Terry made $125 per week.

Beethoven: a large St Bernard, the star of several films in which the Newton family struggle to cope with their boisterous but loving dog. There were six films in the series and even an animated television series.

Benji: there has been a series of films starring the small mutt named Benji, beginning in 1974, and there are plans to make a new film starring 'Benji', a rescue dog who is now the third dog to play the part.

Old Yeller: this 1957 film tells the tale of a young ranch boy who adopts a yellow mongrel dog who helps him through a series of events while his father is on a cattle drive.

Rin Tin Tin: tales of Rin Tin Tin, the German Shepherd dog, have been appearing on the radio, television and film screens since 1918. Rin Tin Tin was a puppy found by an American serviceman in France during the First World War and taken back to America. He found the dog was able to perform many tricks and so put him forward for film auditions. His first starring role in a film came in 1923 and he then appeared in more than 10 films and starred in several radio series from 1930 until 1955. There have been several generations of Rin Tin Tin and the current dog, the 10th in line, still makes public appearances. The original Rin Tin Tin received a star on Hollywood's walk of fame.

Other dog film stars include:

- Einstein, the first dog to time travel in the *Back to the Future* movies.

- Skip, the Jack Russell Terrier from *My Dog Skip*.

- Hooch, who starred alongside Tom Hanks in *Turner and Hooch*.

- Shadow and Chance in the two versions of *Homeward Bound* (more recently called *The Incredible Journey*).

Doggy films to come out in the last few years have included *Bolt, Snow Dogs, Hotel for Dogs* and *Marley and Me* (based on the best-selling book).

Doggy Oscars

Dogs even have their own awards ceremonies to attend:
- *The Fido Film Awards, first held in London in 2007. Winners have included the corgis who played* the Queen's pets in The Queen, *starring Helen Mirren. Poppy, Anna, Alice, Oliver and Megan, won the 'Best Historical Hounds' and 'Best in World' awards.*
- *The Palm Dog award, held during Cannes Film Festival since 2001.*

🐕 ON TELEVISION 🐕

Man's best friend is also often a star of the television screen. Here are some favourites.

Eddie from *Frasier*: Eddie the Jack Russell Terrier owned by the character of Frasier's father Martin was a firm favourite on the show. He was known for tormenting the main character, Frasier, and would often stare at him for hours. The part of Eddie was played by two dogs – Moose and his son, Enzo.

K9 in *Doctor Who*: K9 is the robotic dog companion of Doctor Who. He has appeared in the series on four different occasions (as four different models) and also appears in the spin-off series *The Sarah Jane Adventures*. He is known for his catchphrase 'affirmative' and there are plans for him to star in his own series starting in 2009.

Sweep: The grey-haired, long-eared doggy companion of Sooty is a well-loved British television star and is perhaps best known for his distinctive voice: a high-pitched squeak.

Celebrity trainers for problem dogs

Victoria Stilwell, star dog trainer of the reality TV show It's Me or the Dog *on Channel 4 comes clad in ominous black to help owners with problem dogs. Through every episode, she trains the dog, achieving success-story behaviour, while millions watch to judge and condemn the faulty dog owner. Stilwell makes no bones about her opinion that problem dogs arise because of the owner, not the dog.*

Wellard and **Betty** in *EastEnders*: Two of the most beloved additions to Albert Square in recent years have been Betty, a Cairn Terrier owned by the character of Pauline Fowler and Wellard, the Belgian Tervuren, who has been owned by Robbie Jackson, Gus Smith and Tiffany Jackson. Wellard's character won the award for 'Best Pet' at the Digital Spy Soap awards and one of the dogs who played Wellard, Kyte, has appeared in films such as *102 Dalmatians* and *Gladiator*.

The *Blue Peter* dogs: The children's TV programme has owned a total of eight dogs over the years, as well as helping with the training of several guide dog puppies. The first dog to appear on the show was a mixed-breed female called Petra, who had a litter of puppies while on the show, including one called Patch who would himself become a *Blue Peter* dog. Another family team to appear on the show were the Golden Retrievers Goldie and her daughter Bonnie. A memorable member of the *Blue Peter* family was a Border Collie called Shep, who most people remember as the dog who inspired the catchphrase, 'Get Down Shep!'

Dogs in advertising

Several companies have made dogs the face of their brand over the years and some of the most memorable have included:

- **The Andrex puppy**: *Andrex have used a puppy in their adverts since 1972 and the lovable Labrador has featured in over 120 adverts.*
- **Volkswagen Polo advert**: *featuring a Jack Russell Terrier singing the song* I'm a Man, *the advert was banned after the RSPCA complained of animal cruelty.*
- **The Dulux dog**: *Dulux paint have been using an Old English Sheepdog in their adverts since the 1960s. Many people actually refer to this breed of dog as a Dulux dog rather than a sheepdog.*
- **Churchill**: *The nodding toy Bulldog used by the Churchill insurance company has become a favourite thanks to his catchphrase 'Oh yes!'*

🐕 IN ANIMATION 🐕

The most common appearance for a dog on television tends to be in the form of an animated character. Here are a few memorable cartoon canines.

- **Gromit**: Gromit is the long-suffering canine companion of Wallace, the wacky inventor created by Nick Park. The two Aardman animation characters have appeared in a series of clay animation short films including *The Wrong Trousers*, *A Close Shave*, *A Matter of Loaf and Death* and a full length-film called *The Curse of the Were-Rabbit*. The characters are modelled from plasticine clay and are filmed using stop motion animation. Every part of a scene, including the characters, sets and props are positioned and a picture is taken. The whole scene is then repositioned very slightly and another picture taken. This series of pictures gives the impression of motion and makes up the film. This painstaking technique is very time consuming and it can take a whole day to make just one second of film. *The Curse of the Were-Rabbit*, for example, took five years to film. The adventures of Gromit and his master Wallace have won several Academy Awards, including the award for best animated short film. Gromit has no mouth and so makes his feelings known through his extremely expressive eyebrows. Gromit is often seen knitting and drinking tea with his master, when he isn't getting him out of scrapes that is! Gromit often helps Wallace with his inventions and he has a Double First in Engineering for Dogs from Dogwarts University.

- **Snoopy**: Charlie Brown's pet beagle has become one of the most beloved comic characters in history. His antics of sleeping on the roof of his doghouse, dressing up as a pilot and always trying to kiss Lucy make him a lovable beagle for everyone.

- **Scooby Doo**: the cartoon series following the cowardly Great Dane Scooby Doo and the Mystery Inc gang has been running in various forms for nearly 40 years and has even been made into three live action movies with a computer generated Scooby. Scooby Doo's involvement in solving mysteries while always snacking on 'Scooby snacks' and being afraid has made him a much-loved character for generations. The show also featured his puppy nephew, Scrappy Doo.

- **Muttley**: the sniggering mongrel sidekick of Dick Dastardly in the *Wacky Races* cartoon series.

- **Santa's Little Helper**: Bart Simpson's Greyhound first appeared in the first full-length episode of *The Simpsons* aired on television. He is adopted by the family after Homer loses the Christmas present money by gambling on him at the races. The dog loses and is kicked out by his owner but is adopted by the family as their Christmas present.

- **Brian Griffin**: the talking Beagle from the TV hit *Family Guy* is not your usual cartoon canine. Brian loves to drink martinis dry, and he's a gifted writer who contributes for *The New Yorker*. He went to an Ivy League university, he reads Richard Dawkins for fun, drives his own car, and pays his own bills. He occasionally dates women.

- **Huckleberry Hound**: a Hanna-Barbera character, this southern hound's television show was the first animated show to be nominated for an Emmy.

- **Goofy**: Goofy first appeared with Mickey Mouse in 1934 (his earlier appearances dub him Dippy Dawg) and had his first solo appearance in 1939. He is known for being clumsy and has a distinctive laugh and yell.

- **Pluto**: while Goofy walks upright and talks, Pluto is definitely a dog. He is Mickey Mouse's pet and had his first comic appearance in 1931. He differs from other Disney characters in that he cannot speak but often uses his expressive ears and face to communicate.

- ***Dogtanion and the Three Muskehounds***: this Spanish cartoon from the 1980s tells the tale of Dumas' *Three Musketeers* but casts dogs in the roles of the main characters. The show was produced in Japan and although broadcast there first, it was dubbed in Spanish. The show first appeared on the BBC in 1985.

🐕 IN THE SPOTLIGHT: 🐕 CELEBRITY DOGS

The first dog in the White House: as part of the hype surrounding US President Barack Obama's settling into the White House, there was much talk about the First Family's choice of dog, following the promise Obama made to his daughters during his campaign that he would buy them a puppy. There was some speculation that the chosen dog would be a crossbreed, possibly a Labradoodle. A crossbreed (or 'mutt,' as Obama has called himself) would have reflected Obama's own mixed racial heritage.

The Obamas' final choice, however, was a purebred Portuguese Water Dog named after the musician Bo Diddley. Bo was a gift to the Obama girls from Senator Edward Kennedy and was apparently chosen as he would be less aggravating to Malia Obama's allergies.

Although Bo is now the 'First Dog', he is not the first dog in the White House. Bill Clinton had a chocolate Labrador called Buddy and George Bush had a Springer Spaniel named Spot, one of the puppies his father's dog Millie had while she was First Dog in the White House.

Pickles, the World Cup saviour: Pickles the dog found the lost football World Cup trophy after it was stolen in 1966. Just four months before the World Cup was due to begin in the host country for 1966, England, the Jules Rimet World Cup trophy was stolen from an exhibition in London. A blackmailer was eventually arrested, but the trophy remained missing.

A week later, Pickles, a mongrel out on his neighbourhood walk, sniffed it out from under a parked car where it was wrapped in newspaper and showed it to his owner, David Corbett. Corbett's ensuing visit to Scotland Yard brought him and Pickles media fame. Dog and owner became TV stars, and Pickles starred in a comedy movie called *The Spy with the Cold Nose*. When England won the World Cup, Pickles was invited to the celebration banquet and got to lick the plates clean.

Bob the Parliamentary candidate: Bob was a Springer Spaniel who stood for election in 1982 as a representative of the Monster Raving Loony Party.

Tobey the millionaire: the richest dog in the world has to be Tobey, a Poodle who was left $75 million in his owner's will.

Unending loyalty

Greyfriars Bobby is an example of a truly loyal companion. After his owner died Bobby went to his graveside in an Edinburgh churchyard every day for 14 years, until his own death in 1872. There is now a statue of Bobby as a memorial to his unending loyalty and several films have been made about him.

WORLD RECORD HOLDERS

- The tallest living dog is Gibson, a harlequin Great Dane from California, measuring 107cm tall on August 31, 2004.

- The world record for the highest jump cleared by a dog is 172.7 cm, achieved by Cinderella May, a greyhound of from Miami, Florida, USA. This was measured at the Purina Incredible Dog Challenge National Finals, Gray Summit, Missouri, USA on October 7 2006.

- A Lhasa Apso named Word was held on doggy death row for a total of eight years and 190 days. Word was initially incarcerated at the Seattle Animal Control Shelter, USA on May 4, 1993 following two biting incidents but was released on November 10, 2001 where he was transported to the Pigs Peace Sanctuary, Washington, USA.

- The world record for the most tennis balls held in the mouth by a dog at one time is five. Augie, a Golden Retriever owned by the Miller family in Dallas, Texas, USA, successfully gathered and held all five regulation-sized tennis balls on July 6, 2003.

- The fastest time a dog has unwound a non-electric car window is 11.34 seconds and was achieved by Striker, a Border Collie from Hungary. The record was set on September 1, 2004 in Quebéc City, Canada.

🐕 IN WARS 🐕

There have been some notable heroes among dogs who have served in war.

- Just Nuisance is the only dog to have been officially enlisted in the Royal Navy and was given full military honours when he died.

- Judy, a dog serving in the Royal Navy, is the only animal to have been recorded as a Japanese prisoner of war.

- Seargeant Stubby served during the First World War and is the most decorated service dog.

🐕 IN SCIENCE 🐕

Dogs have played a part in some key scientific breakthroughs in history.

Pavlov's Dog: Pavlov, the Russian scientist, discovered the theory of classical conditioning while studying dogs' saliva. He found that the dogs were salivating before the food was in their mouth and through a series of experiments conditioned the dogs to associate the sound of a bell with receiving food. Eventually the dogs would salivate at the sound of the bell alone. Pavlov was awarded the Nobel Prize in 1904.

Space Stars: Strelka and Belka were the first two Sputnik dogs to return alive to Earth. They were sent by a USSR space mission in 1960. The dogs were accompanied by a rabbit, mice, rats, flies, some plants and fungi. The whole crew went into space and came back safely – and in harmony. Belka later had a puppy called Pushinka, who was presented by Soviet Premier Nikita Khrushchev to US President John F. Kennedy. Through the tensions of the Cold

War, Pushinka found a sweetheart with a Kennedy family dog called Charlie, and had four puppies that JFK called 'pupniks.'

Marjorie: in 1922 a dog without a pancreas was crucial in the discovery made by Canadian scientists Fred Banting and Charles Best of the role of insulin in controlling diabetes.

> *Pocket fact* 🐾
>
> *In 2005 an Afghan Hound in South Korea named Snuppy was the world's first genetically cloned dog.*

🐕 IN OUR LANGUAGE 🐕

Have you ever realised just how much you mention dogs on a daily basis? Even non-dog lovers will regularly refer to canines in every-day speech.

Dog days: a way of trashing hot, humid weather through July–September. The name comes from the ancient Egyptians, Greeks and Romans. They thought that the Dog Star, Sirius, which rises with the sun at this time of year, joins forces with the sun to make humans prostrate and lazy.

Raining cats and dogs: some believe that the saying relates back to Norse weather lore, when rain was equated with cats, and wind with dogs. It is also thought that the phrase could date back to medieval times when during heavy rain the corpses of cats and dogs would be washed through poor drainage systems. There is also the possibility that the phrase stems from the time when most cottages had thatched roofs, allowing animals to crawl in to take shelter, only to be washed into the house during heavy rain.

Dog's dinner: this phrase is generally used to refer to something which is messy. There are many who claim that the origins of this phrase are unknown, while some argue that rather than referring to an unkempt appearance the phrase actually means to be over-dressed (originating from the British army). However, one logical argument states that the phrase derives from the fact that at one time a dog's dinner would be made up of a huge mix of left-overs from human meals and would therefore often end up as a huge mess.

A barking dog never bites: this phrase refers to someone who is always making threats but never actually carries them out. Rather than having specific origins it is simply a description of a certain type of behaviour. It is similar to saying 'his bark is worse than his bite'.

Let sleeping dogs lie: a warning to someone to leave a situation alone as it will only get worse if they get involved. The phrase is a proverb dating from the 13th century and appears in Chaucer's poem *Troilus and Criseyde* (1374) in reverse, ie it's not good to wake a sleeping dog.

You can't teach an old dog new tricks: this phrase means that it will be difficult to teach someone a new skill or a new way of doing something, mainly on account of their age. It is another proverb with unknown origins.

It's a dog's life: this also has some confusion over its meaning. While many take it to refer to a life of hard work (reflecting the labour roles dogs were originally bred for) others think it describes an easy life. It is most commonly accepted that the phrase dates from the 1600s and means a life of hard work and misery.

Dog tired: this is a way to describe total exhaustion and once again has its roots in the hard-working roles dogs used to fulfill in society. The phrase is an Old English one and supposedly refers to Alfred the Great's policy of making his sons chase hunting dogs.

Whichever caught more dogs would be allowed to sit at his father's right hand at dinner, but he would be physically exhausted.

Going to the dogs: this phrase refers to the decline in quality or reputation of something, such as a place or company. The phrase has its origins in China when dogs were not allowed within the walls of a city. Rubbish would be thrown to the dogs wandering outside the walls and anyone banished from the city would literally be 'going to the dogs'.

Barking up the wrong tree: this is used to describe a mistake or error made while trying to accomplish something. Its origins date back to the days when dogs were used for hunting and occasionally a dog would identify the wrong location for the hunted prey.

Dogsbody: refers to the working origins of dogs. A dogsbody is someone who performs a menial task, essentially a servant. This term is also a rank in the Royal Navy for a junior officer, originating from the horrible food the sailors were served on ships in the 1800s and was later applied to the lower ranking officers.

Hair of the dog: used to describe an unusual hangover cure. The hair of the dog suggests having more alcohol as the cure for a hangover. The expression comes from an old treatment for rabies which directed that hair from an infected dog should be placed in its wound. The phrase, as we know it in reference to a hangover treatment, was used in Shakespearean times and is also a common phrase in Hungary.

Every dog has its day: using this proverb means you are expressing a belief that everyone has one day where everything goes right and they are a success.

Sick as a dog: an expression that describes someone who is extremely ill. The phrase dates from 1705, when it was first recorded, and seems to refer to the fact that as dogs will eat almost anything they are often spectacularly ill.

Dog eat dog: this expression is used to refer to harsh competition, one in which there is no mercy shown. Nowadays it is commonly used to refer to business and workplace competition. The phrase comes from a Latin mis-translation (dog will not eat dog) and dates from the 18th century.

🐕 IN ART 🐕

- The earliest examples of dogs in art are cave paintings discovered in Spain which are thought be over 12,000 years old.

- Samples of art from some ancient civilisations show the presence of dogs in human life.

- Paintings from Egypt, sculptures from Assyria (in modern Iraq) and mosaics from the Romans all depict dogs in various shapes and sizes, including mythical dogs like Anubis and Cerberus.

- Hunting dogs appear alongside Harold on the Bayeux Tapestry.

- In Jan van Eyck's famous Arnolfini Portrait (1434), particular care was taken to include the couple's little pet dog.

Pocket fact 🐾

Queen Victoria's mother commissioned a portrait of the young queen's Cocker Spaniel, Dash, as a gift for her 17th birthday. Victoria is known to have commissioned several other dog portraits throughout her lifetime.

- In the 18th century dogs were most likely to be included in the great hunting portraits fashionable at the time.

- George Stubbs painted the first portraits of single dogs in the 1770s.

- Modernists make use of dogs and Picasso is known to have included them in his paintings.

- The painting of *Dogs Playing Poker* by Coolidge is one of the most famous representations of dogs in art and is part of a series of 16 paintings depicting dogs engaged in human activities.

Art for art's sake?

In 2007 artist, Guillermo Vargas photographed an emaciated street dog chained up for three hours in Nicaragua as an art exhibit. This caused much anger, as the dog allegedly starved to death. The artist refused to comment on the dog's fate. From his point of view, his exhibit showed how no one cares about a dog dying on the street, but put it in a frame and people start to care.

🐕 IN QUOTES 🐕

'Aristocrats have heirs, the poor have children, and the rest keep dogs.'

Spike Milligan

'Nothing but love has made the dog lose his wild freedom, to become the servant of man.'

D H Lawrence

'Agreeable friends – they ask no questions, they pass no criticisms.'

George Eliot

'If your dog doesn't like someone you probably shouldn't either.'

Unknown

'Whoever said you can't buy happiness forgot little puppies.'

Author, Gene Hill

'The more people I meet the more I like my dog.'

Unknown

'Buy a pup and your money will buy love unflinching.'

Rudyard Kipling

'It is scarcely possible to doubt that the love of man has become instinctive in the dog.'

Charles Darwin

'Histories are more full of examples of the fidelity of dogs than of friends.'

Alexander Pope

'You think dogs will not be in heaven? I tell you, they will be there long before any of us.'

Robert Louis Stevenson

'If you eliminate smoking and gambling, you will be amazed to find that almost all an Englishman's pleasures can be, and mostly are, shared by his dog.'

George Bernard Shaw

'To his dog, every man is Napoleon; hence the constant popularity of dogs.'

Aldous Huxley

'To sit with a dog on a hillside on a glorious afternoon is to be back in Eden, where doing nothing was not boring – it was peace.'

Milan Kundera

'You want a friend in Washington? Get a dog.'

Harry S Truman

🐕 IN JOKES 🐕

How do you catch a runaway dog?
Hide behind a tree and make a noise like a bone.

What dog loves to take bubble baths?
A shampoodle.

Why did the snowman call his dog Frost?
Because frost bites.

What do you get if you cross a dog and a lion?
A terrified postman.

A man went to the zoo.
When he got there, there was only a dog.
It was a pretty shitzu.

What do you call a dog with no legs?
It doesn't matter what you call him, he isn't going to come.

What's the difference between a new husband and a new dog?
1. After a year, the dog is still excited to see you.
2. A dog only takes a couple of months to train.

Why did the poor dog chase his own tail?
He was trying to make both ends meet.

What happened when the dog went to the flea circus?
He stole the show.

What happens when it rains cats and dogs?
You can step in a Poodle.

What happened to the dog that ate nothing but garlic?
His bark was much worse than his bite.

What did the dog do when a man-eating tiger followed him?
Nothing. It was a man-eating tiger, not a dog-eating one.

What did the dog get when he multiplied 497 by 684?
The wrong answer.

Which dog can tell the time?
A watchdog.

Which dog looks like a cat?
A police dog in disguise.

Why are dogs such poor dancers?
They have two left feet.

Why did the dog say miaow?
He was learning a foreign language.

3

OWNING A DOG

🐕 FACTORS TO CONSIDER 🐕

Before you run out to buy your perfect puppy there are a few serious considerations to make before you decide to own a dog. These include factors like cost and time but also your dedication and lifestyle: do they suit dog ownership?

Time: do you have the time to properly care for a dog? Dogs need regular exercise and can live for 15 years or even longer. Are you ready for such a long-term commitment? If you buy a puppy you will need to dedicate long hours to training it and will not be able to leave it alone for long periods of time.

A dog is for life: not just for Christmas

This phrase was coined by the RSPCA to try to combat the influx of abandoned dogs into shelters which occurs around February or March, when the novelty of a puppy Christmas gift wears off.

Money: dogs can be expensive to own. There may be the initial cost of your purebred puppy and then there are veterinary costs (such as vaccinations and check-ups), licence fees, food costs, kennel fees (if you need to go away), grooming costs and any repairs to damage which may be caused. Pet insurance is highly recommended to help alleviate costs in the event your dog becomes ill or has an accident.

Pocket fact 😺
People in Wales and northern England are the most likely to own a dog.

Lifestyle: does your lifestyle suit being a dog owner?

● Is your home big enough to house your chosen breed?

● Think about the possible size your chosen breed can grow to. They won't be a puppy for ever.

● Is there enough space for your dog to run around or is there somewhere nearby you can take it for a walk?

● Will you be home enough to play with your dog? Dogs get lonely easily and this can lead to behavioural problems.

● Do you have other pets or children? You will need to choose a breed known for its ability to get along with children and other animals and carefully train it.

● Before you bring your new dog home you will need to 'dog-proof' your home. It is much like having a new baby so you need to be sure there are no cables or wires (puppies love to chew these) and remove any furniture or carpets you don't want chewed or which your puppy might have an accident on.

You need to be sure you can change your lifestyle to suit your dog, not the other way round.

Robodog

If you wanted a pet dog who would need no feeding, training and cleaning up, AIBO (Artificial Intelligence roBOt, a homonym of 'buddy' in Japanese) would have been the choice for you.

Launched by Sony in 1999 (and discontinued in 2006) AIBO boasted canine body language. AIBO could fetch a ball, stretch or jump around the room. It could also interact with about 100 voice commands delivered by its owner.

🐕 CHOOSING YOUR DOG 🐕

WHICH BREED?

You have to decide which breed best suits you and the needs of your family. See p.10 for more about breeds.

Pocket tip 🦴

Keep in mind that as a general rule, purebreds will be more expensive than crossbreeds and mixed breeds.
For example:
- *A Labarador puppy can cost £300*
- *A Staffordshire Bull Terrier puppy can cost £395*
- *A Sharpei puppy can cost £600*
- *A Chihuahua can cost £900*

Obviously the cost will vary depending on where you buy your puppy but if you want to be sure you are getting a purebred make sure you buy from a reputable breeder who has evidence to back up your puppy's lineage.

WHERE TO CHOOSE FROM

Where people in the UK get their dogs from	
Rescue home	32%
Friend/family	25%
Recommended breeder	16%
Private ad	16%
Internet	8%
Pet Shop	7%

Rescue home

It's popular, and helpful, to get new dogs from a rescue home, which brings with it its own challenges. For reliable rescue homes you can ask at your local council or look up the dog charity 'Dogs Trust' (tel 020 7837 0006; www.dogstrust.org.uk).

If you choose to get your dog from a rescue shelter there are a few factors to consider:

- Make sure you ask for any information about the dog's breeding or lineage.

- Ask if the dog is fully grown.

- Ask why the dog was given to the rescue centre in the first place. You will need to know about any behavioural problems before you get home to be able to handle them effectively.

- Does the dog have any health problems?

- Does it look healthy and active?

If you adopt a dog with behavioural problems (which can range from urinating in the house to separation anxiety to aggression) you will need to be prepared to learn the proper techniques to deal with these behaviours and have the patience to work through the problems. Although there can be extra work involved, adopting a dog from a rescue centre can be an extremely rewarding experience.

Breeders

To ensure you choose your puppy from a responsible breeder, ask a vet or friends for recommendations. Unscrupulous breeders might pawn off a puppy from a puppy mill, where the creatures may be kept caged like chickens in a coop. The cramped space does no good to the temperament of such puppies, and even if they look healthy, there's no guarantee that they don't carry inherited dog diseases like hip dysplasia.

Internet

Buying a dog on the internet may seem like an easy and fun idea. You type 'puppies for sale' into a search engine and hundreds of adverts selling adorable puppies appear. The internet is a great place to do your research and it can help you to find reputable breeders or rescue centres.

There are several problems that come with buying a puppy online, though. Most puppies available over the internet come from puppy mills. Some puppy mills keep their dogs in terrible conditions and more often than not the puppies are ill as the sellers are able to avoid health regulations by selling their animals over the internet.

Use the internet for your research and to find reputable breeders but be very cautious about buying a dog online.

Pocket tip 🦴

You should never buy a dog without having seen it first yourself.

Pet shops

Unfortunately most pet shops present the same problems associated with buying a dog on the internet. Most of the puppies in pet shops come from puppy mills and unlike breeders, pet shops will be looking to sell the puppies while they are at their cutest, with no regard for whether the buyer will make a good owner.

Pet shops are a great place to buy supplies but you should approach buying a dog there with caution. Do your research and find out if the pet shop you intend to buy from has a good reputation with breeders and find out if they offer any advice or help once you have purchased your dog.

From friends or family

Adopting a dog from friends or family can be a good option, although there are a few things to bear in mind. One advantage can be that you know at least one of the parent dogs well and will be able to decide whether that breed and their behaviour suit you. There are a few things you should consider though:

● Do the parent dogs have any health or behavioural problems? Friends or family may not be as able to discuss this as well as a recognised breeder.

● Make sure you are buying the breed that is right for you, not just choosing this breed for the sake of convenience.

● There may be some awkwardness over the price. Some puppies can fetch a high price so you should establish early on whether this dog is a gift or a purchase.

Pocket tip ✒

If you do decide to adopt a dog from family or friends make sure you don't take the puppy away from its mother before it's ready. Puppies should stay with their mother until they are seven or eight weeks old.

🐕 NAMING YOUR DOG 🐕

Not every dog is called Rover or Spot. The most popular names in the UK in 2008 were:

- Alfie

- Barney

- Cassie

- Charlie

- Jake

- Jasper

- Jess

- Lily

- Max

- Meg

- Millie

- Molly

- Murphy

- Poppy

- Sam

When naming your puppy:

- Keep the name simple. A name of one or two syllables makes it easy for your dog to recognise your call. Or if you *must* have a longer name and shorten it, make sure the nickname remains consistent.

- If you have more than one pet, make sure their names sound different enough that they can tell the difference. Make sure that the dog's name doesn't coincide with family members or close friends either.

- Choose a name that you would like to call. It may be clever to trash your hated politicians by giving your dog their names, but remember you have to live with your pooch for its lifetime.

- Avoid a name that sounds too close to the commands 'Sit', 'Come', 'Down', 'Fetch', 'Stay', and 'No'.

Pocket fact 🐾
Writer Salman Rushdie named a Bulldog 'Jawaharlal' after the first prime minister of India in The Moor's Last Sigh.

STRANGE DOG NAMES

Since the 1990s, the likes of Britney Spears, Posh Spice and David Beckham have unwittingly lent first names or nicknames to canine kin. Of course celebrities can use other celebrities as inspiration for their pet's name– hence TV and radio personality Sara Cox has a dog named after the rap star 'Snoop Doggy Dogg'.

These dogs have had to be very tolerant of their owners' tastes:

- Big Nose

- Bowchickawowwow

- Brittany Hillary Candy Princess Pop Star

- Chickens

- Deeohgee

- Havoc

- Joe Cocker

- Moo
- Omelette
- Wart

Pocket fact 🐾

The '90s explosion of the internet spawned cute Dachshunds called 'Dot-com' and nowadays there is a growing number of dogs called Google.

TEACHING YOUR DOG ITS NAME

- Look at your dog and say its new name in a voice of enthusiasm.
- When your dog answers your look (which will likely be often) offer a food treat and praise.
- Repeat this procedure over days until your pet gets the hang of it.

🐕 THE COST OF A DOG 🐕

Owning a dog can be very costly – more expensive than owning other pets such as a cat or rabbits. Are you prepared to pay anything up to £9,000 over your dog's lifetime?

BREAKDOWN OF COSTS

Dog itself: anything up to £1,000 (depending on the breed)

Registration with Kennel Club: approximately £50

Vaccinations: up to £70 each time, without insurance

Pet insurance: anything up to £200 a year

Food: anything from £100 a year (depending on the size of your dog)

In addition to these essential costs there are other expenses to keep in mind:

- Kennel fees

- Training or behaviour classes

- Bedding and toys

- Identification collar and lead

Pocket fact ❦
In 2008 the average annual cost of owning a dog was £502.

🐕 WHAT DOGS EAT 🐕

ORIGINS OF DOG FOOD

For centuries dogs lived as meek scavengers of table scraps (meat and bones and stale bread). Now, the dog food section of the supermarket is vast, and many dogs get a more balanced diet than their owners do.

Dog biscuits were invented in the 1860s. Like many great scientific discoveries, it all started with an accident.

According to one story, an enterprising London butcher tried to reinvent himself as a baker by creating a new recipe for biscuits. After his first batch failed, he tried out a biscuit on his pooch, who loved it. So the butcher started selling dog biscuits to country gentlemen for their sporting dogs. The idea caught on so well that an American businessman acquired the butcher's recipe towards the turn of the century and sold it across the Atlantic.

According to another story, the American James Spratt was selling lightning rods in London when he was offered some mouldy ship's biscuits for his dog, and he invented a concoction that would please his own pet better.

Pocket fact 🐾

Jennifer Aniston was made to eat a dog biscuit on the German TV show Wetten, dass. . .? *Aniston wasn't pleased: 'It's horrible what we feed animals and they look forward to that – it's a treat for them!'*

- Between 1907–1908 the US company FH Bennett Biscuit Co. set up a dog biscuit company with the brand name Malatoid. This biscuit morphed into 'Milk-Bone,' which dominated the US dog biscuit market until the late 1960s. In the 1970s more manufacturers added their products to the market and nowadays there is a very wide choice.

- In the United States after the First World War, horses and mules were replaced by cars and tractors for transport. Canny businessmen began to sell horseflesh as canned food for dogs. This trend, begun in the 1920s, grew rapidly through the 1930s when there were about 200 brands on the market.

- In the 1940s, the canned food market slumped because of the Second World War. There was less horseflesh around and canning was expensive with the rising cost of tin. But manufacturers found the potential of bonemeal, which could be used for 'dry' dog food.

- In the late 1950s, the Ralston Purina company developed different kinds of dry 'dog chow' which were sold through grocery store chains in America. In the 1970s, the same company developed 'moist' kinds of dog food for those who didn't like dry dog food.

What's in dog food?

The dog food that you can buy from your local supermarket or pet shop consists of basic ingredients such as corn, wheat, barley, rice or soy meal, individually or in combination. Commercial dog food often also includes meat like beef, lamb, chicken, liver or meat by-products.

There are a few basic types of commercially produced dog food:

- **Dry**: known as kibble, you have to add water before your dog can consume it. This is usually the cheapest variety of dog food.

- **Semi-moist**: cooked combinations of soybean meal, fresh meat or meat by-products, sugar, animal fat, preservatives, and substances that allow the product to stay moist without spoiling. The dough is moulded into shapes resembling meaty chunks, but since dogs are attracted to the smell and taste rather than the sight of food, the fake meat probably pleases the owner rather the dog.

- **Wet/canned**: usually expensive and spoils easily.

- **Frozen**: less common than the other varieties of food. Made with raw, uncooked meat, frozen dog food contains no artificial preservatives. It skips the processing that the above varieties go through, conserving the original nutrients. Frozen foods generally have a sweetener that adds to their calorific value, which helps dogs with a physically active lifestyle. These foods have to be kept frozen until used, and the unused remainder must be kept in the refrigerator.

What are meat by-products?

*You might have read this on your dog's food label.
By-products are parts of animals that humans would not
normally eat, such as feathers, feet, beaks, cheek meat, tail
meat and wool.*

*By-products, to be useful to your dog, have to be processed
properly before their nutrients can be absorbed. A lot of
people might find the idea of eating chicken beaks and
feathers strange (even for a dog), but in a processed form they
are good sources of protein.*

SPECIAL DIETARY REQUIREMENTS

Dog food is available in forms that cater to various dogs' special
dietary requirements. There are different kinds of food available
for growing puppies, adult dogs, aged dogs, sporting dogs, show
dogs, pregnant and lactating dogs – you name it, there will be dog
food to cater for your dog's needs.

- Dogs that are allergic to the common ingredients corn, wheat and
  chicken can get food with substitute starches for the grain and
  'novel proteins'. The substitute meat ranges from the usual beef,
  lamb (or even white fish) to unconventional venison and duck.

- Vegetarian dog foods are for dogs whose owners do not want
  them to consume meat products, as well as for dogs who have
  experienced allergic reactions to a number of animal-based
  ingredients. 'Natural' food is available without chemical
  preservatives. There's no standard definition of 'natural' in
  dog food, so it can sometimes mean 'organic' food. Organic
  food includes grains grown without pesticides and chicken or
  beef raised without antibiotics and hormones, and fed only
  grains grown without pesticides.

- Vitamin-rich food exists, with Omega 3 and Omega 6 fatty acids for the health of a dog's coat and skin. There's also a good chance you'll find added anti-oxidants and herbs in your dog's food.

HOW TO CHOOSE FOOD

- Dry food is cheaper than the other varieties, per pound.

- Dry food is more convenient to store. Canned food, once opened, has to be used up quickly.

- Canned food can include as much as 75% water and colour enhancers like iron oxide and sodium nitrate. This does not provide a balanced diet for a dog.

Apart from the moisture content of the food, you have to consider the quality and quantity of the food. High-quality foods are likely to cost more, but dogs tend to eat less of them. High-quality foods are also produced by companies where researchers are constantly coming up with new formulas to suit dogs' nutritional needs.

Often, the label of the food product will advertise the nutritional content with the claim that it's a 'complete food.' A dog food is really 'complete' not by boasting a flood of nutrients, but by having them in a form that the dog's systems can absorb. High-quality dog food generally has nutrients that can be readily absorbed.

Pocket tip ✔

For a dog with allergies or dry skin, serve an Omega fatty acid supplement.

- Read the product label with care to check the nutrients.

- Choose the food based on how physically active your dog is. Avoid food with a high fat or carbohydrate level if your dog likes to sleep a lot, or if your children share their snacks with it. Try to avoid protein above 25% for puppies and above 22% for dogs who are moderately active.

- For dogs, looks mean little. Smell and taste mean much. A can with yellow carrots and green beans will please you, but not necessarily your pet.

- 'Natural' food can mean a lot of things in the canine world – there's no accepted definition yet. It can mean organic grains and an organic meat source. It can also simply mean food without artificial preservatives.

- Different breeds of dogs need different kinds of food. Some dog foods do cater to the different nutritional requirements of large, medium and small sized dogs.

Pocket fact 🐾

Most dogs will stay healthy on a diet of good-quality kibble, garnished with meat broth without salt, vegetables, and scraps of lean meat. Remember that like humans, dogs need a balanced diet of proteins, carbohydrates, fats, minerals and vitamins to keep their bones and muscles in good condition.

HOMEMADE FOOD

You can choose to feed your pet a selection of cooked meat or raw meat, meaty bones, chopped vegetables, and multivitamin supplements. Either way, remember that dogs aren't too particular, so they won't turn their noses up at leftovers.

The Pocket Bible dog food recipe

You will need:

- 500g beef mince (or chicken, lamb or turkey)

- 200g of rice
- 1 carrot finely chopped
- 1 courgette chopped
- 1 stick celery finely chopped
- 1 butternut squash
- 1 tsp chopped parsley

Boil the rice. Chop the vegetables. In a separate pan, fry the beef mince for five minutes on low heat.

When the rice is done, add the vegetables and simmer for two minutes, stirring all the time. Pour the rice-vegetable mixture in to the frying pan with the beef and stir. Add the parsley.

Cool for at least an hour before adding the mixture to your dog's dry food (kibble) — and dish up.

Makes one serving.

Bones and Raw Food

BARF (Biologically Appropriate Raw Food) is the 'ethically sourced' food of the canine world. The BARF philosophy comes from a book written by Australian vet Ian Billingshurst, called Give your Dog a Bone *(1993). Billingshurst urged dog owners to feed their pets the bones and uncooked food that their ancestors had been eating for years before the appearance of commercial dog food.*

- *A BARF meal consists of uncooked meaty bones and uncooked meat (often from fish carcasses and chicken necks and backs), raw eggs, vegetables, fruit, yogurt, cooked cereals, and cottage cheese. Grains are excluded.*

- *BARFers think that commercial dog food does not provide balanced nutrition so they add herbs, enzymes and other supplements to the dog's diet.*
- *They point out that their meals are more interesting to the dog as a BARF diet offers variety by including seasonal foods.*
- *According to BARFers, the bones-and-raw-food diet helps dogs live longer, stink less and become more lean and springy.*

But BARF has its critics:
- *Some think BARF is a passing fad, with nicknames for its acronym such as 'born again raw feeders'.*
- *Some vets and health experts assert that dairy products are not good for an adult dog. They also advise against feeding raw meat, which may have a high fat content.*
- *Bones and raw meat may contain parasites like E. coli and salmonella, which can infect humans and other animals. Although dogs themselves might stay unaffected and the majority would not exhibit symptoms, they can pass on the organisms to other animals, or humans.*

SERVING FOOD

- Feed your dog on a fairly regular schedule, with two meals a day. Let the feeding schedule be a relaxed one, though regular.

- Use a standard food bowl that is easy to keep clean. Make sure the bowl is clean before and after meals, and keep checking it for mould.

- Put the food and water bowls in an elevated position rather than directly on the floor. This puts less strain on your dog's front end and makes eating more comfortable.

- Feed your dog in a place with no distractions. Keep young children away so that your dog doesn't have to struggle for its food.

- Make your dog sit before you serve the food. This will ensure that it will eat quietly and won't spill food all over the floor.

- Give your dog about 15–20 minutes to eat. After that, remove the food bowl.

- If you have more than one dog (or more animals than one dog), feed them separately, at a distance of two feet or so.

Happy Birthday!

What do you treat your dog to on this momentous day? Not cream cake! It's bad for your dog, and they probably won't enjoy it all that much either.

Try a fresh and warm meat pie instead. How about a low-fat, alcohol-free, guiltless shepherd's pie? Instead of candles, insert beef sticks, which means your dog will have something better to do with the 'candles' than simply blow them out!

WATER

Let your dog have access to cool, fresh water throughout the day. But if you are feeding dry food, restrict the water supply immediately before and after meals. This will prevent dry food expanding in your dog's stomach to cause bloating.

Normally, the crunchiness of dry kibble is good for teeth and gums. But if your dog likes its kibble softer, you can soak it for 10–15 minutes before serving it.

WHAT YOUR DOG SHOULDN'T EAT

The following is a list of foods your dog won't actually die from eating (unless it positively hogs them down), but which aren't good for it. You need to make sure your dog's health does not suffer through these foods.

● Grapes and raisins

● Vegetables like potato, mushroom, onion and garlic

● Raw fish and raw eggs

● Dairy products like milk and cheese

● Tobacco

● Alcoholic drinks

● Food and drink with caffeine like coffee, tea, and chocolate

---

Chocolate can kill dogs. True or false?

True – partly. A dog shouldn't gobble down 20 Easter eggs, but one won't kill it. Chocolate contains theobromine (a xanthine compound in the same family as caffeine), that is toxic to dogs in sufficient quantities. It takes a fairly large amount of theobromine (100–150mg/kg) to cause a toxic reaction, although there are variables to consider like the individual sensitivity, animal size and chocolate concentration.

● Be aware that 1.1kg of milk chocolate or 146 grams of cooking chocolate can kill a dog weighing 22kg.

● Milk chocolate and white chocolate are less dangerous to your dog than cooking chocolate.

Pocket tip

Just remember the fate of poor Wellard, the dog in EastEnders, when you feel like sharing that chocolate bar with your dog. A post mortem of poor Wellard revealed a telltale chocolate wrapper.

Eating grass

While there's nothing to worry about if your dog eats grass, make sure it doesn't do so immediately after insecticides, herbicides or other chemicals have been applied to the grass. The label on the product would probably caution you about this too.

🐕 HEALTH AND MAINTENANCE 🐕

VISITS TO THE VET

You should take your dog to the vet at least once a year for a check-up. If your dog is elderly or has special medical needs then you need to visit more often.

It may be that your vet will find a problem before you do, and catch the problem before it gets serious. Remember, prevention is always better than cure. The vet will check:

- Vaccinations: the annual vaccinations your dog needs should include distemper, leptospirosis, and parvovirus. In case you have travel plans, ask your vet about bordatella ('kennel cough') – it'll be relevant whether you're travelling with your dog or whether you board it in a kennel.

- Behaviour: if you've noticed signs of unusual behaviour in your dog, such as excessive barking or ripping the sofa, tell your vet.

- Fleas, ticks, and worms: flea larvae are born survivors and can live all year round in your home, even if they don't seem to be bothering your dog at the moment. Fleas can trigger tapeworm infection in your dog, and that needs to get detected early.

- Dental care: your dog will get a dental check-up and possibly have its teeth cleaned. You can also check with your vet if the dental care regime you follow at home for your dog is a good one.

- Older dogs: an elderly dog may have special requirements. It's possible that your dog might develop chronic issues like osteoarthritis, sight or hearing loss, or memory loss. These can be handled by alterations in your dog's lifestyle, and your vet will be able to offer guidance.

PET INSURANCE

It's all very well to scrimp and save wherever possible, but your dog's health really isn't a good place to start. If the time comes when your dog needs a major operation, whether it's post-car accident or for a collapsed lung, you will be eternally grateful that you stowed away that little bit just in case.

Pocket tip

Shop around for the best deal, and check what is covered. Insurance is readily available and you can even pop it in your shopping basket at the supermarket.

- Dog insurance starts at as little as £15 a month. Obviously this covers money towards vet bills, but there are other benefits too, like money to offer as a reward if your dog goes missing, boarding fees, and even death benefits. Even the lowest insurance packages offer respectable benefits, but it is worth getting something slightly more expensive, say for an older dog, in case the vet's bills escalate and exceed the price covered by cheaper packages.

- When calculating insurance prices, insurers generally just want to know the breed and age of your dog, and where you live. It's a good idea to go on price comparison websites to make sure that you get the best deal and find the package that suits you and your dog best. If you have more than one dog, there are sometimes discounts offered for insuring them all with one provider.

Potential dangers for dogs

- *Electrical wires: many dogs, particularly puppies, like to chew wires. To avoid electric shocks and burns, stow wires away from their reach, or at least fastened with duct tape.*
- *Household cleaners: keep these out of your dog's reach. If your dog has swallowed a cleaning liquid by mistake, read the label at the back of the product. It might advise that you need to make your dog throw up. This is not advisable with all products, since throwing up can irritate the dog's oesophagus. You can make the dog throw up by putting your finger down its throat, if it allows you to do so. Otherwise, a hydrogen peroxide solution should do the trick (one tablespoon per 30lb of your dog's bodyweight). You should also take your dog to the vet as soon as possible.*
- *Rat poison: the red and green pellets look and taste gratifying to rats, and unfortunately to bigger animals as well. If your dog eats some, call the vet immediately. Rat poison will cause your dog to bleed through its orifices, and if not treated immediately, will cause death. If your dog eats a dead poisoned rat, the effect will depend on how much poison the rat consumed. Call your vet for advice.*
- *Houseplants: some plants are poisonous to dogs and can lead to illness or death. Plants to beware of include philodendron, azalea and rhododendron.*
- *Medicine: keep this out of your dog's reach.*

GROOMING

Grooming helps remove your dog's dead hair. Brushing distributes natural oils through the body and keeps your dog's skin and coat healthy.

It also gives the opportunity to run your hands over your dog's body to check for telltale lumps and bumps, and to make sure that your dog isn't carrying too much extra weight.

Pocket fact ❧

Scientific studies show that grooming helps reduce stress for both you and your dog. It's a soothing act for you both, and quality time spent together.

You need different kinds of grooming techniques for dogs with different lengths of hair.

Smooth coat (such as Beagle, Dalmatian)

A brush once a week is sufficient to remove shed hair and dead tissue. Use a rubber brush to remove dirt and loosen shed hair, and clean out the dirt and hair with a bristle brush. A smooth coat should be sleek and shiny.

Long coat (such as Maltese, Collie)

Dogs with long coats are prone to matted hair, and need more frequent grooming. A long coat needs daily grooming. First, detangle matted hair with a comb or pinhead brush. Don't cut out matted hair with scissors. Use the comb to shape the hair, with attention to the tail and legs. Trim straggly hair.

Short coat (such as Chihuahua, Miniature Pinscher)

Dogs with short hair still need grooming, but less regularly. A pinhead brush will remove knots and mats. Then, a bristle brush will remove dirt and dead hair. Don't cut out matted hair with scissors.

Pocket tip 🦴

Dogs with long hair between their toes shouldn't have their hair clipped. Clipping may be essential for large mats in the dog's hair which can't be removed by scissors — but if you are in any doubt, ask a professional groomer.

Silky coat (such as Afghan, Yorkshire Terrier)

You need to groom a silky coat a few times each week. First, detangle with a comb or pinhead brush. Then use a bristle brush. Make a centre parting and brush downwards on both sides of your dog. Trim straggly hair.

Why is my dog licking itself so much?

Self-preening is a means of relieving stress for anxious dogs. Talk to your vet about this if you are really concerned.

If your dog grooms itself too much, it can develop a skin problem like 'acral lick granuloma' on its elbows and legs. It's similar to bed sores in humans and looks like an ugly wound. The problem is not life-threatening, but it's a good idea to talk to your vet about it.

NAIL CARE

Your dog doesn't need its nails clipped that often. A dog that walks on hard surfaces, like pavements, will have its nails worn down naturally. But when you hear a distinct 'click-click' patter as your dog walks on the floor, it's time for a pedicure. If nails aren't clipped in time, they can break, bleed or grow into your dog's foot.

How to clip your dog's nails:

- Buy nail clippers specially designed for pets.

- Seat yourself and your dog on the floor.

- Hold your dog's paw and push on the pad gently to make the nail protrude. Clip from the end of the nail.

- Stop when you reach a black dot in the centre of the nail. This dot is the 'quick' which contains nerves and blood vessels, and will bleed profusely if you cut it by mistake. On white nails this dot is pink. If you cut into the quick by accident, press with cotton wool. If the bleeding doesn't stop, talk to the vet.

- Make sure you clip the dewclaw, which is situated towards the inside of the leg. In many dogs dewclaws are snipped off after birth, but in case they aren't, remember that the dewclaw can curl and grow into the surrounding soft skin.

Pocket tip 🦴

Get your dog used to nail-trimming from the puppy stage. Train your puppy by holding its paw and then rewarding it with a food treat. This will cause much less stress when you have to clip the nails for real. Your puppy may have nails too soft to trim, so use a human nail file instead. The same sort of file will also work for dogs with nails that are brittle.

BATHING

- Get a dog shampoo, preferably something mild and all-purpose without perfume or chemicals. Don't use human shampoo because your dog's skin has a different acidity.

- Get something to bathe your dog in – preferably a plastic bucket or a tub, and line it with a floor mat so that your dog won't slip. This should work for small dogs, but for large dogs you might want to bathe them outdoors with buckets of luke-warm water.

● Fill the bucket or tub with lukewarm water and lower your dog into it.

● After your dog's fur is wet, apply the shampoo, making sure that it doesn't get into the eyes and earholes. Lather all over. Rinse off with jugs of lukewarm water or a shower nozzle, avoiding the eyes and earholes.

Dogs have an instinct to dry themselves after a bath by shaking themselves or rolling on the ground, even on the grass. To avoid having to give your dog another bath, lay some towels beforehand on the floor for your dog to roll on. You can lend a hand with a towel, but make sure you stand well away when your dog shakes itself dry, or you'll get soaked. Some dogs will willingly submit to a hair dryer.

Pocket tip 🦴

Many dogs patter around with an unpleasant aroma after a bath, until you are left wondering why you went through all that trouble in the first place. Don't worry — the smell will wear off when your dog dries thoroughly, and you will be left with a sweetly scented creature.

TEETH

A dog needs nearly as much dental care as you do. Most dogs over three years of age have dental issues.

Ideally you should brush your dog's teeth on a daily basis (this will help with plaque and bad breath) but most people tend to brush at least three to four times per week. Use a canine toothbrush and an enzymatic canine toothpaste which comes in various flavours. Don't use human toothpaste.

Apart from regular brushing, keep checking for bad breath, broken or missing teeth, and check that there are no swellings on the jaw. Alert your vet if you see anything suspicious. A good vet will perform a dental check-up on every visit anyway.

- Get your dog used to the habit of having its teeth brushed from the puppy stage, before it loses its milk teeth (between four and six months). First, when your puppy is in a quiet mood, wipe its teeth with gauze. It will get used to you handling its mouth. Reward your patient puppy with praise and a treat.

- Move on in time to a soft toothbrush. Dip the brush in luke-warm water, and then brush gently at an angle.

- When your dog is fine with a toothbrush, only then use toothpaste.

Pocket tip 🦴

Some dogs can never be coaxed into accepting a toothbrush. Talk to your vet about other options. There are oral gels, dental pads for gums, and chewing cleaners that will massage gums and keep the teeth healthy. Dry dog food also helps keep teeth and gums healthy by scraping away debris between your dog's teeth.

A CANINE MAKEOVER

Dog salons, or professional dog grooming parlours, are becoming increasingly popular in the UK. You can now get your dog groomed by an expert with a degree in animal care.

- Professional groomers can often deal with finer points of grooming that might make you nervous. Your dog may have a coat that's hard to brush, and excessive matting that, if not detangled, can exacerbate matting in the surrounding hair.

- The groomer will brush and detangle your dog's coat thoroughly.

- Its nails will be trimmed, its ears will be cleaned, and straggly hair will be plucked before a nice warm bath.

- Some breeds like Bichon Frisés and Poodles don't moult naturally, so they need regular visits to a professional groomer.

Of course, the grooming is about looks too, so parlours usually offer a choice of styles for a long-haired dog, ranging from the traditional to the trendy.

The price depends on where the parlour is and what it offers, but usually ranges from £50 to £70.

Usually, owners can stay and watch while the dog is being groomed. You can take this opportunity to ask the groomer for helpful tips. Many parlours also offer dog-sitting services though, in case you have things to do while your dog is fussed over.

🐕 INFESTATIONS 🐕

WORMS

Worms are present in most puppies from birth, so when you have a new one, you should take it to the vet to set up a de-worming regime for the whole year.

The most common worms present are tapeworms, roundworms and hookworms. Every repeat visit to the vet will give a chance to evaluate the de-worming regime.

Signs of a worm infestation:

- A good appetite, but loss of weight

- Stomach upsets

- Weakness and ennui

- A pot belly

Remedies

Fortunately, worm infestations are easy to treat, as long as your dog is not too ill.

- Tell your vet, who may suggest a stool test. Worm eggs can be identified in the sample.

- Get rid of the stool when your dog goes to the loo outdoors. This will help prevent a re-infestation of your dog, and protect other dogs. Some worms can infest humans too.

FLEAS

Fleas live all year round in our homes, so action can be taken only when they really manifest themselves in your dog.

Pocket tip

If your dog is suddenly going bald and scratching all the time, fleas, ticks and lice are a very likely cause. Beware especially of fleas, which are associated with tapeworm infestations.

Precautions you can take:

- Be especially careful in summer and autumn. Fleas thrive in hot and humid environments. Hoover your house thoroughly and often, with special attention to nooks and corners. Dispose of the vacuum cleaner bags carefully, as fleas can live and reproduce in them.

- Call a professional exterminator to get rid of flea infestations.

- Trim garden hedges and mow the lawn.

Signs to look out for:

- Your dog will keep biting its tail or rear end, and scratching itself all over. There may be raw patches on the skin.

- Brush your dog over a white sheet. If black specks (of digested blood) fall off, you have a sure sign. But don't get worried. There are many ways to combat the fleas.

Remedies

There is a range of flea control products available on the market. Some inhibit flea growth and reproduction, some kill flea larvae and some kill grown-up fleas.

- Shampoos, sprays and powders often contain growth inhibitors.

- The efficacy of flea collars depends on the dog's size, kind of coat and the chemical used.

- Your vet might prescribe a pill.

- Home remedies include brewer's yeast, garlic, vinegar and kelp.

- There are flea repellent insecticides, but these are going out of fashion.

- Groom your dog with a fine-toothed comb, and drown the fleas you find in soap water.

- Bathe your dog every week.

- Wash your dog's bedding every week.

Pocket tip 🦴

You can also get special shampoos and powders for ticks and lice as well.

🐕 STERILISATION 🐕

This is a topic that gives rise to much controversy. Rescue homes and dog charities usually play it safe by sterilising their dogs, but it's really up to you to decide whether you'd like to avoid trouble altogether or prepare for a litter in the future.

THE PROS

A spayed female dog won't:

- Drop spots of blood on furniture and carpets during menstruation.

- Get pregnant.

- Suffer maternity-related complications.

- Have a litter of puppies you don't want (remember, many puppies are abandoned to the streets every year, which results in overcrowding at rescue shelters).

- Have cancer in her reproductive organs.

- Have a dangerous womb infection called pyrometra.

- Need to be separated from male dogs in heat.

- Have mood swings when in heat.

- Have false pregnancies.

- Have complications with her heat cycles if she has diabetes.

A neutered male dog won't:

- Get testicular cancer.

- Get tumours like anal adenomas.

- Have prostate gland issues.

- Get into fights with other male dogs.

- Have a tendency to stray in the search for a mate.

- Mount humans, animals and objects.

THE CONS

- It is possible that a sterilised dog will put on weight.

- The dog's coat might become coarser.

- Female dogs may start bed-wetting habits.

- Some argue that it's unfair to deprive a dog of sexual choice – and that we humans shouldn't make the decision for a different species.

If you decide to keep your dog intact, you have to:

- Prevent situations where pregnancy can occur.

- Be on the watch for cancer or infection.

Pocket tip

There is a kind of chemical contraception available for dogs, but it is administered by injection and is very painful.

🐈 TAIL DOCKING 🐈

Cutting off the organ of a living animal sounds like the height of cruelty, but docking dogs' tails is an old convention that has recently become a controversial topic.

Tail docking was traditionally performed on around 50 breeds with long tails at birth, such as the Doberman Pinscher. The reason for this is that docking avoids tail damage: when hunting dogs move through heavy shrubbery, their tails can get snagged and consequently, tear and bleed. For the same reasons, in the past working terriers have had their tails docked. When they dig into the earth, having a docked tail helps them move through small spaces.

However, tail docking can be seen as animal cruelty. In the UK, tail docking by anyone other than a vet has been illegal since 1993. The Animal Welfare Act of 2006 contains a general ban of tail docking for England and Wales, with the exception of working dogs or when the procedure is needed for medical reasons. The Animal Health and Welfare Act 2006 in Scotland also includes a ban on all non-therapeutic tail docking of dogs.

Tail docking is still a hotly debated issue: how can vets know the dog will be used as a working dog at the time of docking? It is the discretion of the individual practitioner, and so some continue to dock tails where appropriate, while others feel the practice is unethical and constitutes animal cruelty.

Pocket fact 🐾

Some European countries, such as Sweden, forbid docking, while others, such as France, still allow tails to be docked.

Post-operative care

When your dog has surgery, your vet will advise how to take care of it, with the right medication and list of check-up dates. But it helps to keep these simple tips in mind as a general rule:

- *Your dog will usually take 24–48 hours for recovery, and it will spend most of this time sleeping. Keep your dog's bed in a room with a comfortable temperature, where children or other animals won't step in to disturb.*
- *Your dog may feel nauseous due to the anaesthesia when it wakes up. Serve a light meal of easy-to-absorb fish or chicken. Provide fresh and clean drinking water all day.*
- *Keep the bandages dry. Whenever your dog goes outdoors, fix a plastic bag over the bandage, or get a drip bag which is more durable. But remember to remove the plastic bag as soon as your dog comes indoors, otherwise moisture will make the wound fester. Keep an eye out for discharges or smells in the bandage area and alert your vet if you see anything suspicious.*
- *Keep an eye on the stitches. Tell the vet if you see a swelling or discharge. For some stitches you will have to go back to the vet to have them removed, while some stitches will dissolve into the skin.*
- *In the days following the operation, take your dog outdoors for minimum exercise and to go to the loo. Keep your dog on a lead. Discourage running, jumping and bounding up and down a flight of stairs.*
- *Fix a plastic 'Elizabethan' or 'Buster' collar to your dog to prevent licking or scratching over the operated area. The funnel-shaped collar should be worn constantly if possible, especially at night when you can't keep an eye out for any scratching. Make sure that it fits well and doesn't obstruct eating or drinking water.*

🐕 WEIGHT ISSUES 🐈

According to a study by the vet charity PDSA, one in three dogs today is overweight. Overweight dogs can fall victim to diabetes, arthritis and kidney problems – all of which could cut your pet's life short in one way or another. A sagging Labrador can lose as much as two years from its normal lifespan.

Pocket fact 🐾

Overweight dogs are growing at an alarming rate: in 2006, 21% of dogs in the UK were considered overweight, increasing to 30% in 2007.

Studies show that pets are often obese in places where humans share the trait. The Midlands, with the highest human obesity figures, sadly shows canine obesity figures of 29% in 2007. Dog obesity stood highest overall in the north-west at 31%. As someone once put it: 'If your dog is fat, you're not getting enough exercise.'

WHAT TO LOOK FOR

A healthy dog's ribs can be easily felt, and its waist and tuck-up (the area between its ribcage and its rear end) are visible without being protruding. There should be a thin layer of fat between the ribs.

- An *overweight* dog will have a spongy layer of fat over the ribs, and an invisible waist and tuck-up.

- An *obese* dog will have thick fat on its ribs, along its spine and around its tail.

- A *very obese* dog will have a paunch on its belly, and deposits of fat throughout its body.

Causes of obesity

- Too many calories. Your dog's mealtimes might have the calories spooned out, but you may not know when it's noshing on the sly.

- Spaying or neutering can in some cases pile on the pounds. The procedure can be responsible for hormone changes and a lower metabolic rate, which may lead to exercise and calories going out of sync. Some owners therefore avoid sterilising.

- Food treats are a good way to train a puppy, but should not continue into adulthood. Replace food treats with gentle praise as a reward.

BACK TO FITNESS

- Take your overweight charge to the vet so they can tell you how much your dog should ideally weigh. Now both of you must work out a food-and-exercise regime that won't stress your dog out.

- Unless you're totally feeding your dog homemade food, go for dry dog food. Although the higher-quality dog food is more expensive, your dog will eat less of it, so it will be cost-effective. Your dog will also get the required amount of proteins, carbohydrates, fats, vitamins, and minerals.

- Stop your dog eating on the sly. Having your child learn social skills by sharing that Digestive biscuit with your dog is a good beginning, but not a long-term project. Curbing random treats is good for the health of your dog.

- While you cook, eat and wash up after your meal, don't look your dog directly in the eye, and deafen your ears to its whines. If necessary, shoo your dog to its bed while you eat.

- Never underestimate the necessity of fitting your dog's food to its level of physical activity. Make sure that your walks together add up to a few miles every week.

- Exercise through long walks, play sessions, and general running around. Making them chase or fetch an object is usually a challenge they're happy to take on.

- If you have two dogs, or have a neighbour with a friendly dog, set up joint play sessions. A dog unwilling to exercise by itself may very willingly tone its muscles via playful rivalry with another dog.

Pocket tip 🦴

To treat your dog to a snack, give it slices of apple, banana or orange.

Don't overdo obesity control

Your dog won't reach a normal weight overnight. Any fitness regime takes time and patience, and before you embark on a fitness regime with your dog, consult with your vet about an exercise programme that will keep your dog physically fit, but not stress its heart and lungs, or bring on muscle strain and pain.

When switching from one kind of food to another, watch out for alterations in your dog's physical activity, coat texture and general health.

🐕 EXERCISE 🐕

Everyone knows that you need to exercise your dog regularly – and it's probably going to be a good old walk. Here are some general tips to get you and your dog moving:

- Don't exercise your dog immediately before or after it has had a meal, or else it may have a stomach upset. Provide a small amount of water to drink just before and after exercise.

- Different breeds need different amounts of exercise. Often this is a reflection of the original roles they were bred for. Pastoral or herding breeds like games of fetch. Terriers like to dig for mice and rabbits. Hounds like short spells of intensive exercise.

- A dog needs exercise no matter what the weather. In winter, ice, snow and de-icing salt may have got trapped in your dog's feet, so wipe the paw pads when you come back. In the summer, be wary of heatstroke and sunburn. Hot pavements can damage your dog's feet.

- Avoid rough play that will strain your dog's bones and muscles. Build in a warm-up and cool-down period to your exercise routine.

Pocket tip 🦴

Regular exercise is important for your dog even if it suffers from arthritis or hip dysplasia. Work out an appropriate exercise programme with your vet.

- With a puppy, go slowly at first with the exercise, and then build up gradually. At the beginning, let your dog run on soft surfaces like sand, grass and earth until its feet pads become tough.

Greyhound exercise

Since Greyhounds are the track stars of the canine world, they need to be monitored carefully when they switch to the life of a family pet. A recent retiree from the race tracks might run into walls and trees. To get your retired Greyhound used to the boring everyday world, keep it on a lead in open spaces. If you have French doors or large windows in your house, your Greyhound may try to bound through the glass and injure itself. Try putting stickers on the patio doors at your dog's height, so that it can see when the doors are closed.

WALKIES!

How far you walk your dog will depend on their size, age and fitness level. Obviously a larger, active dog like a Collie will need a longer walk than a Chihuahua. Here are a few tips to help you have an enjoyable walk and to make sure you stay in control. You want it to be that you take your dog for a walk, not the other way round.

- Try to have the walk at approximately the same time every day. Once your dog gets used to the idea, it will fetch its lead to remind you at the right time.

- Make your dog stand still while you put its lead on. You need to make sure your dog knows who's in charge.

- When you get to the front door make sure you go out first and make your dog wait inside for a few seconds.

- Don't let your dog walk in front of you. Keep them at your side in a 'heel' position.

- Ensure your dog is wearing an ID tag on its collar in case it gets lost.

Pocket tip ✔

Carry poop scoop bags with you. One of the big responsibilities of being a dog owner is to clean up after your dog in public spaces. According to a 1996 law, owners can be prosecuted if they don't clear up dog mess in designated areas.

- Try to keep the walk fun, and don't let it become yet another chore – especially if you don't like long walks yourself. Keep varying the route, and keep some time aside for play.

- When you get back from your walk give your dog some water to drink.

Is it a good idea to exercise your dog while cycling?

Cycling with your dog is fine as long as you take the proper precautions. Luckily dogs have an instinct to chase anything moving, so training them to run beside you while you're on a moving bike isn't a problem. Begin by cycling slowly while your dog walks, and then pick up speed so that your dog can break into a run. Make sure not to overdo it though.

You do have to make sure that your dog runs straight and doesn't cross from side to side, otherwise you might run over it. Train your dog by keeping it tight on the lead while you cycle slowly at first. Your dog will soon get the idea and then you can let the lead go loose.

Using a lead

Keeping a lead on your dog gives you control over a walk or a run. Since 2006 there have been Dog Control Orders which allow local authorities to designate areas where dogs must be kept on a lead. These areas are usually signposted and there can be a £1,000 fine for failing to follow these regulations.

Only let your dog off the lead if they have been properly trained. You need to be sure they won't run away or be aggressive towards other dogs or people. There are several training methods you can use to make sure you can let your dog off its lead safely.

Pocket tip 🦴

Keeping your dog on its lead is especially important if you walk your dog through the countryside. Do remember that farmers have the right to destroy an animal that disturbs farm animals.

If a farm animal happens to chase your dog, let your dog off the lead, otherwise you might both end up getting hurt. The same applies when you walk through a wildlife area, where you need to make sure your dog stays away from birds' nests.

If your dog runs away while it's off the lead, don't give chase. It will think it's a game and keep running. Stay still and call it back to you.

When walking your dog in a public place, make sure it has a collar with your name and address (including the postcode), otherwise you might get fined up to £5,000.

Pocket tip 🦴

Look for a lead made of leather or fabric. Rope or chain versions can cause blisters on your hand if your dog pulls hard.

If you have a puppy try to get a harness-type lead rather than one that goes round its neck. You don't want to strain its neck because you are pulling at the lead trying to train it.

Ever wondered what dog collars looked like in the past?

Visit the amazing collection at Leeds Castle in Kent, with a display of nearly a hundred collars dating from five different centuries. You might feel glad that you and your dog didn't live in the 15th, 16th or 17th centuries when hunting dogs wore collars with imposing spikes to protect them from bears, wild boar and wolves in the forests.

SWIMMING

Most dogs love swimming, but make sure that the water is warm rather than cold, since cold water will constrict your dog's blood flow close to the skin, and make the muscles less effective. If you live in a cold climate don't let your dog in the water in the cold winter months and make sure they don't stay in too long when it's warmer.

Swimming is a very intensive exercise for dogs – five minutes of swimming equals a run of five miles—so make sure the water doesn't fool them into splashing around too much.

Dog spa day

Dog spas will offer luxury swimming for your dog, as well as a day of relaxing hydrotherapy for dogs that may need it. Often you will find them integrated with grooming parlours.

A day at the dog spa might mean a swim in an indoor heated pool, as well as other doggy beauty treatment packages. These packages, priced according to the services offered, range from a paw pedicure to teeth brushing to a stress-relieving massage. The staff are experienced at handling dogs, so you can leave your dog to have fun free of worry.

GAMES

Training for agility trials (a doggy version of a hurdle race) is not the only way to have fun whenever you spend time outdoors with your dog. There are other simple sports that you can play at the local park.

- Frisbee.

- Dog diving – for dogs who like swimming, retrieving a toy thrown in the water can be great fun.

- The classic game of 'fetch', although avoid throwing sticks, as the wood can splinter and damage your dog's teeth and insides.

Pocket tip ✔

Dogs who like retrieving will love to play hide and seek with you when you take cover behind trees and bushes.

- Training to obey orders such as 'stay' and 'heel'.

- Doggy dancing, or 'heelwork to music', is a recently developed dog training sport. Dog and owner interpret a piece of music of four minutes' duration, and co-ordinate their movements into a dance routine. A great place to watch is at Crufts where the best doggy dancers in the country show off their moves.

The fun of Frisbee

Frisbee with dogs shot into popularity in 1974, when an American college student, Alex Stein, jumped the fence at a major baseball game with his dog, a Whippet called Ashley. Ashley amazed crowds with eight minutes of continual Frisbee-catching, leaping nine feet into the air and running at a speed of 35 miles an hour. The baseball game was stopped as commentators switched attention to the Frisbee.

🐕 COMMUNICATION 🐕
AND BEHAVIOUR

When a well-mannered dog is referred to as 'man's best friend' it's not only the dog's loyalty that earns it kudos but the fact we can communicate fairly well with our canine companions, unlike many other pet animals. Hold a beloved terrapin in your hand and it will show little interest, and guinea pigs squeak only when it's lunchtime. But your dog, and its woofs, whines and yaps, will express a thousand emotions – friendly or otherwise.

Pocket fact 🐾

Dogs have about 100 facial expressions – most of them done with an artful lift or drop of the ears.

Dogs have fewer vocalisations (about 10) than cats and other animals, but are able to communicate quite expressively using their tails, ears and other bodily gestures.

They rely mostly on their sense of smell to understand the world around them, so once a dog has decided he likes your scent he will remember you when you next meet.

Most of the body language expressed by dogs communicates either dominant or submissive messages and it's useful to bear this in mind when trying to figure out what your dog is trying to tell you.

Pocket tip 🦴

It's important when looking at canine body language to consider what the dog's whole body is doing, not just its head or tail. So if a dog's tail is wagging hard check it is not also showing its teeth as a sign of aggression: in this case the wagging tail would be a sign of excitement not happiness.

BODY LANGUAGE

Here's a rundown of a few common doggy body language signals and what they mean:

Tail

- **High tail**: a tail held high in the air means the dog is alert.

- **Tail between legs**: this gesture means the dog is afraid or anxious.

- **Bristled tail**: this means the dog is ready to defend itself against an aggressor.

- **Small, slow wags of the tail**: this tail movement means the dog is unsure of the situation.

- **Fast, large wags**: this is one canine bodily behaviour most people are familiar with. It means the dog is happy or excited.

Mouth

- **Showing teeth**: while some people think this looks like a dog is smiling it can actually be a show of aggression and should be treated with caution. If the dog is showing only its front teeth this can be taken as a submissive gesture but if a dog is showing most of its teeth it is a sign of aggression.

- **Licking mouth**: if a dog licks its mouth when there is no food present this is a sign that the dog wants to be left alone.

- **Licking**: dogs tend to lick people and other dogs they are familiar with as a form of greeting.

Ears

- **Erect and forward**: this is a sign of attentiveness.

- **Laid back**: this is a negative or fearful signal.

Head

- **'Eyebrows'**: dogs have a ridge above their eyes which acts in the same expressive manner as a human's eyebrows. They raise their 'eyebrows' to show interest, raise one to show surprise and will lower them when angry or frustrated.

- **Tilted head**: a dog tilting its head to one side is displaying curiosity.

Dog greetings

When meeting another dog a dog will first assess whether the other dog is friendly by whether it barks first. If the initial encounter is not aggressive, dogs will then move on to greet each other by sniffing the other. If this encounter goes well the dogs will then play with each other or show some sign of affection like licking or wagging their tail.

When you are meeting a dog for the first time it is best to kneel down to their level (so you don't appear dominant or aggressive) and offer your hand to be sniffed. Don't shove your hand in the dog's face but let it come to you. Keep your hand in a loose fist with the back of your hand facing the dog. Look out for any signs of aggression and be ready to pull your hand away so it doesn't get bitten.

If the dog sniffs your hand and appears friendly you can move on to pat them, but make sure you pat their chest or shoulders first, as patting their head can seem like an aggressive gesture. The dog should remember your scent the next time you meet so a quick sniffing assessment should be enough.

BARKING

Alongside their body language, barking is a dog's main form of communication. Dogs will bark to communicate something (such as 'there's someone at the door'), to gain attention or when they are excited or playing.

Pocket tip ✒

It is important when trying to understand your dog that you pay attention to both their body language and their barking.

There are different tones to dogs' barks; they are not merely noises. A short, higher pitched bark means the dog is playful or excited, whereas a low, unmodulated bark means the dog is warning of a disturbance.

Dogs will mainly bark to convey an alarm or a warning, or during play. They will also use a series of growls, howls, whines and whimpers to communicate.

Bowlingual

In 2002, a group of Japanese inventors won the Ig Nobel prize (a parody of the Nobel) for 'promoting peace and harmony between the species' through a toy that translated doggy emotions into human language.

The toy was manufactured by Takara Toy Company and called 'Bowlingual'. It read a dog's emotions from its bark, and classified these emotions into one of six categories: happy, assertive, frustrated, sad, needy or on guard. Then the toy selected a funny phrase to correspond with the emotion. So you would have moments when your dog would confess — straight to your face — 'How boring' or 'I can't stand it' or 'You just don't get it'.

How does the toy work? A radio microphone is attached to the dog's collar, which picks up the dog's bark and transmits the sound to a hand-held receiver. The receiver matches the sound to a computer database of thousands of dog barks. Then it displays the dog-talk on an LCD screen.

The toy makers claimed that Bowlingual could interpret the barks of over 50 breeds of dog, ranging from German Shepherds to Chihuahuas. However, they also added the caution that the toy was for 'entertainment' and not an exact reflection of the dog's feelings.

Foreign barks

Although in English we use the word 'woof' to represent a dog's bark (or sometimes 'ruff') there is a variety of other words used throughout the world:

English: woof woof
Dutch: waf waf
Danish: vov vov
Finnish: vuff
French: ouah ouah
German: wau wau
Greek: gav gav
Hebrew: woof woof
Hungarian: vau vau
Italian: bau bau
Japanese: wan wan
Russian: hav hav
Spanish: guav guav
Swedish: vov vov
Turkish: huav huav

🐾 FAMILY INTRODUCTIONS 🐾

DOGS AND CATS

Dogs and cats have been called 'natural antagonists'. A cat will usually react to a dog by acts of aggression, such as a hiss or a swat with its paw. It may also try to run away or hide from the dog, and might spray to alert the dog to its 'territory'. Dogs with hunting origins such as terriers will chase cats instinctively and may react aggressively to a hostile cat.

If you are introducing your new dog to a home where you already have a cat you will already have picked a dog breed with a reputation for getting along with cats. Even so, your cat needs to build up its courage around the dog, and this may call for considerable time and patience.

Pocket fact 🐾

In January 2008 a dog called Arthur warmed animal-lovers' hearts by an act of grave-digging. It was so distressed at the death of its old companion, a cat called Oscar, that it retrieved the corpse from its burial-spot in the garden. Arthur certainly isn't the first dog who has loved a cat, but it's important to remember that fairytale friendships like this need lots of hard work and wisdom. One false step, and a lifetime of work can be undone.

Meeting for the first time

- Select a room that is not the cat's 'territory', that is, not the room that contains your cat's bed, food bowls and litter box. Shut the doors and windows of the room, so that your cat cannot run away when it sees the dog. Make sure there is something high for the cat to jump up on, like a scratching post, a bookshelf, the window sill or the back of a sofa.

- Bring in the dog now and keep a hold of it. Most likely, the cat will jump up to a higher position.

- After a few minutes take your dog out of the room.

- Repeat these meetings, keeping them short but frequent.

Living together

- Pay attention to both pets as often as possible. Often your attitude and attention are enough to prevent serious rivalries or hostilities from developing.

- Give quality time to both pets. Individual attention will keep rivalries at bay.

- If the dog ever makes a move to chase the cat, tell it off with a strong 'No'.

- Tell the cat off if it tries to pounce on the dog's tail.

- Give treats to your cat after meetings with the dog, so that the dog's presence feels auspicious to the cat.

- Feed the cat and the dog in separate spaces, so that they don't dip into each other's bowls. Cat food is not supposed to be eaten by dogs, nor the other way round.

- Make sure the cat has a space that the dog can't access, where it can eat or drink water quietly, and have its own litter box. Ensure that the litter box especially is beyond the dog's reach. Dogs can have disgusting habits and may try to eat what's in the box.

- Never leave the cat and the dog alone together until you can be totally sure that they'll behave well without your supervision.

DOGS AND KITTENS

Introducing dogs and kittens is often easier, as kittens haven't learnt the adult ways of their species. Again, introduce them through short but frequent spells and leave them alone together only when they are absolutely fond of each other – a bite or a swat from a dog could kill your kitten! Dogs often like to carry kittens around, but take the kitten away at these moments as the dog's grip might be too strong.

DOGS AND OTHER DOGS

The 'rules' for introducing dogs to each other aren't that different from dogs to cats. Make sure each has its own bed, and acclimatise them to each other through short and frequent meetings at the beginning.

DOGS AND CHILDREN

A dog in the family is great for a child to learn how to care for another living creature.

The child benefits socially, the dog is happier by living in company and they can both stay physically healthy too. Children who have grown up with dogs are less susceptible to allergies from pet fur and their mutual play and exercise helps keep obesity at bay.

This idyllic relationship can only happen though when the child isn't pulling the tail of a long-suffering dog, or when the dog isn't growling at the approach of a toddler who wants a half-eaten doll back.

DOGS AND BABIES

Before the baby comes home

Let your dog have its own space. Move your dog's bed, feeding bowls and toys to an area that the baby can't reach. If your dog hasn't had its own bed before, get one now. Seal off the doggy area with a baby gate. The dog will feel like it has its safe den, and a crawling baby can freely explore everywhere else.

And after

- Offer the dog a treat when the baby is in the same room. It will help the dog think of the baby as a desirable presence.

- Don't pet an anxious dog when the baby is in the same room. Let the dog relax by itself, or wander off, and then cuddle it in a different room.

Pocket fact 🐾

Many dogs become very protective towards a newborn baby and start acting like the nanny. They'll sleep near the cot and signal to you that it's time for the baby's feed, and they'll escort a crawling toddler to make sure it doesn't bump into sharp edges.

As the baby grows

A protective and friendly dog will usually like a child's company, but a curious child may also go overboard and become an irritation.

- In this case it's even more important for the dog to have its own space. Make sure the dog is left in peace during its meals, or when it is sleeping or going to the toilet.

- Let the dog and child spend time together under adult super-vision. Even if the child doesn't tease the dog and pull its tail, a toddler's screams can be frightening. Parents should let the child approach the dog only if the interaction is likely to be gentle.

- Teach the child to stroke the dog where it warms to affection best – on the top of the head and along the back. Reward the dog with praise or a treat for responding to the child. Don't let the child pick up the dog until its arms are strong enough.

- Keep interaction short if necessary. Don't force the child's attention on the dog (or vice versa). Let them grow into tolerating each other.

- Make the child wash its hands after contact with the dog.

- When the child is old enough let them participate in the walking and exercising of the dog, as well as its training.

🐕 OBEDIENCE TRAINING 🐕

Obedience training is important for your dog's social skills. Training your puppy to obey basic commands like 'Sit', 'Stay', 'Come', 'No', 'Down' and 'Off' will make your lives infinitely easier.

WHEN TO START

Training your puppy should begin immediately. Puppies learn best between four and 16 weeks so it is crucial to teach them the rules of the home in this time.

Make sure you have a proper routine for your puppy to help with training. Tell the puppy off if it does something wrong (don't let them get away with it because they're cute) and praise them when they do something right.

One vital training exercise you can undertake in this time is to teach your puppy its name. It's amazing the number of adult dogs who don't respond to their name, only the persistent yelling of their owner!

- Make sure you have your puppy's attention. Say its name clearly and reward it with a food treat when it looks at you.

- Repeat this process several times over a period of time.

- Later replace the food treat with its favourite toy.

Toilet training

It is also crucial to begin house training your puppy as soon as he arrives. Make sure you take your puppy outside regularly to avoid accidents.

- Take the puppy outside as soon as it wakes up.

- Take it outside after playing or exercising.

- Take it outside five minutes after having a drink of water.

- Take it outside 20 minutes after a meal.

Every time you go outside use the same word, such as 'Outside' so that the puppy associates this with going outside and the reward it gets for this behaviour.

Reward the puppy every time it goes to the toilet outside and tell it off if you catch it going indoors.

Pocket tip

If you find an accident inside completely ignore the puppy while you clean it up. It won't make the connection if you tell it off after the event, it will just be confused.

Training with food treats

Food treats are a good way to tempt a puppy into obeying commands. Some trainers think this starts a bad habit, but it's a quick and easy way for you. It's important, however, not to let it continue for long, and so as you reinforce training through the dog's life, keep replacing the food treats with praise and hugs. Eventually, save the treats for special occasions.

Clicker training

You can get a pet training clicker from the pet shop. It's a plastic box that you can fit in the palm of your hand which makes a double 'click' sound when pressed with the thumb. When used in conjunction with food rewards your puppy will soon associate the command with the sound and you can stop using food rewards.

- *Keep a number of treats with you. Give them to your puppy, pausing briefly between each treat.*
- *As the puppy snaps up each treat, click. At some point, the puppy will get the idea that a click means a treat, and is worth working for.*

What should you use as treats?

Use small chunks of food that your puppy can eat quickly and easily, which won't make a royal mess on the carpet, such as:

- *Slices of frankfurters*
- *Cubes of cheddar cheese (remember too much cheese can give them an upset stomach though)*
- *Crackly cereals like rice krispies*

Do count these treats as part of your puppy's daily food ration so that you don't end up with an overweight puppy. Keep in mind that food training is difficult in a family with young children as your puppy might already have access to whatever treats it wants. So do keep children and puppies separate during meals and snacks.

Sit

- Show your puppy a treat. It will try to aim for it.

- Hold the treat in the air above its nose, so that the only way to reach the treat is by putting its rear end on the floor.

- As soon as its sits, click (see p. 128 for 'clicker' information) and surrender the treat. Offer praise.

- After a few tries, your puppy will get conditioned into sitting for the treat. Begin to say 'Sit' when it sits.

- At some point it will all come together in your puppy's brain, and it will sit when told rather than when lured by a treat.

Once the basics are mastered, you can devise your own training exercises for other commands that are unique to you and your dog.

Down

Use this command to signal that your dog should lie down. Use 'Off' when you need to tell your puppy to get off its perch on the sofa.

Come

Reinforce this training command, which your puppy has been learning the basics of since it has learnt its name. Practice the command in a garden, and then in a public park with more distractions.

If your puppy runs away from you in the park, don't give chase – instead, run in another direction yourself so that the puppy comes to you and gets rewarded with treats and praise.

TRAINING CONDITIONS

- Keep it fun. This may sound obvious, but it's easy to forget. Both you and your puppy should go through the training session with a positive mindset. Only train when you're in a good mood, and full of energy. Reserve lots of treats, praise, pats and toys for the occasion.

- Keep the training session short. Puppies have a short attention span and will respond better to three five-minute sessions than a long hour.

- At the beginning, train in a quiet environment with minimal distraction, like a room in your house. Introduce your pup to environments with more distractions gradually – move from the house to the garden, to the public park, and so on.

Pocket tip

If you use a training collar for physical control, never use a chain training or choke collar as you can hurt your dog's neck. Use a halter or head collar instead.

- Expect no miracles. It's impressive that your puppy under-stands you at all! Always finish the session on an uplifting note by giving your puppy an exercise you know it's a master of.

- Associate training with rewards – that's where the treats and pats come in useful. Avoid punishment. If you slap a dog on the snout, it will stop listening to you altogether and may well turn against you. Greyhounds especially are hypersensitive – even a scolding is anathema to them.

Training collar

The simplest collar is the buckle collar. The chain training or choke collar has been widely used but is falling into disuse with the rise of the prong or pinch collar, which sounds and looks cruel but is actually milder in action. The halter or head collar helps the handler to turn the head of the dog rather than its neck.

Despite all your patience, if your growing puppy seems intractable and resistant to learning commands, or growls at you persistently, consider a training class. Don't shout or try to deal with aggression that you can't handle – your action may make the problem worse.

PUPPY CLASSES

If you don't feel totally confident about training your puppy on your own you can take your puppy to puppy training classes. These can be one on one (some trainers will even come to your home) or in groups. Lessons usually cover the basics such as sit, come and stay and will train your puppy not to jump up when greeting people.

There are a few things you should be aware of before taking your puppy to training classes:

- Make sure your puppy is sufficiently bonded with you and your family. You don't want to confuse it by introducing lots of new people all at once.

- Do some research into the types of training methods you would like to use and find a trainer that will follow these methods. For example, would you rather the trainer use a leash or a clicker?

Pocket tip 🦴

Puppy training can be an excellent way of socialising your puppy with other dogs at a young age, meaning they will be better with other dogs when they get older.

Finding a reliable trainer

Ask your vet, dog breeders, staff at the animal rescue shelter, the groomer, or at the pet store. Here are two places to look for reliable trainers in the UK, who can also offer you advice on animal behaviour:

Association of Pet Dog Trainers: tel 01285 810811; www.apdt.co.uk

Centre of Applied Pet Ethology: tel 0800 783 0817; www.coape.org

Take your puppy to a kindergarten only after it has had all its puppy shots. A parvovirus or distemper infection can be fatal to your puppy.

Spend time watching at least two or three trainers before you make a choice.

How to make sure that the trainer is good

- Make sure the trainer isn't pretending to like dogs for money. See how much attention is given to the dogs which don't fit into the group – the overactive ones, the timid ones, and the slow ones.

- The 'Sit' command: this can be the giveaway. The wrong kind of trainer will force the dog into a sitting position by putting pressure on its rear end close to the tail. This shortcut method is unacceptable.

- Test your trainer. Ask what kind of training collar you need. The answer ought to be 'We recommend XYZ but it depends on what your dog needs.' See if the trainer recognises that every dog is different.

🐕 BEHAVIOURAL PROBLEMS 🐕

FEAR

A dog can be fearful by nature or through a bad upbringing, like harsh punishment when it's been trained. Such dogs may be afraid of various environments or events, such as the vet, open or closed spaces, lightning and thunder.

Fear may result in unpleasant behaviour like biting or bed-wetting.

Pocket tip 🦴

Avoid shouting at a dog that's frightened — it will only make the problem worse.

Some fearful dogs can benefit from anti-anxiety medication from the vet, but this can only offer temporary relief. The key point is to make the dog unlearn fearful behaviour. If the root cause is known, a qualified behaviourist will help you go back to the cause and condition the dog into regaining confidence.

If bed-wetting is the problem, you can use dog nappies in the short-term. If the problem is not medical but behavioural, go on a repeat house training programme.

ATTENTION-SEEKING

This can include excessive barking, pawing and jumping, stealing the child's toys, biting at the lead, chasing its own tail, and climbing on furniture when it knows that that is not allowed.

It's common for animal behaviourists to diagnose an unruly dog's antics as attention-seeking. What can the cause be? It could be that your dog is simply bored. Offer attention throughout the day in small doses. Practise spells of seeming neglect. Make no eye contact, don't touch it, and don't talk to it.

If your dog won't get used to being on its own, talk to your vet about consulting a behaviourist, especially if your dog gets aggressive by biting or growling.

EXCESSIVE BARKING

If a well-behaved dog starts forgetting its manners suddenly, find out what the cause could be. Start a diary to record when your dog barks and what kind of sound it makes.

- Could your dog be in pain through illness? A visit to the vet could help sort this out.

- Could your dog be bored? See p.116 for a list of games you could play with your dog that would make for quality time.

- Is your dog lonely? Is it trying to tell you that it needs you? Make an honest appraisal of the time you spend with your dog – do you need to make more time for it?

- If you do spend a lot of time with your dog, is the barking a dependency problem?

Whatever the cause is, there are some things *not* to do:

- If you hit back with a shouting contest, chances are the dog will really think it's a contest, and bark even more to quieten you down.

- Forget those anti-barking collars. When your dog barks, they spray mustard and citronella flavours unpleasant to the doggy nose. Because your dog is clever, it will soon learn that barking makes the air smelly. And it will bottle up its emotions, to be released at another time. Instead of a barking dog, you'll have one who bites. Don't let the barking (which is merely annoying) turn into downright aggression.

Pocket tip

If spending quality time with your dog or a medical check-up doesn't work, consider a visit to an animal behaviourist. Your vet can give you names. Or else get in touch with a qualified trainer. A few simple training exercises can make your dog comfortable with its own company.

DIGGING UP THE GARDEN

Dogs get bored unless they have something to do. A bored dog will make up its own games by digging holes in the garden.

Fence off an area for the dog where it could play king of its own corner. Stress length rather than breadth – it will help the dog run up and down on days when you really, really don't have time to take it for a long walk.

EATING ITS OWN POO

Although this behaviour, known as coprophagia, can be repulsive to the owner, eating faeces is in fact an instinctive behaviour which came from harsher times when dogs ate excrement as a way to absorb as many nutrients as possible. The behaviour is normal, and is practised by other animals such as rabbits.

The simplest way to handle this can be to clean up the poo as soon as your dog is done. Another remedy is to add garlic or canned pumpkin to your dog's diet. The stink might throw the dog off anything with a similar smell. However, this technique has been found to be unsuccessful by some owners as a dog's keen sense of smell means it can simply avoid the faeces which smell like the taste they dislike.

Pocket tip 🦴

It can help to change your dog's diet, by giving them dried foods for example, which are more easily digested and therefore produce less appealing faeces (as there are fewer nutrients).

Another method can be to distract your dog as soon as it has been to the toilet, allow it back in the house straight away and give it a reward when it comes in. Leave the dog indoors while you clean up but don't let it seem like a competition for food as this will only make the behaviour more appealing to the dog.

POSSESSIVE AGGRESSION

Before you think of your dog's biting or growling behaviour as a real aggression problem, eliminate other causes.

- Is your dog in pain? Even a well-behaved dog will lose its temper if you don't pay attention to that festering wound on its ear.

- Young adult dogs, mostly males, will often exhibit dominance-related aggression. Many of them may have been possessive when they were puppies, but that doesn't mean aggression is with them to stay.

If none of these seems to be the cause, you have to think possessive aggression. When a dog adopts a threatening attitude by standing over, staring, snarling or biting when toys, food, or other items in its possession are at issue, it's time to take the following steps.

- If your dog gets angry if approached during a meal, feed it in a separate space.

- If it gets snappy when playing with a toy, make sure that it plays with its toys away from other people or animals.

- A puppy behaving possessively needs to be taught that this behaviour won't be allowed. Teach the dog a training command to drop objects. Start with boring objects. Make the dog move away from the object and reward it with a treat and praise. Proceed to more interesting objects — let the reward take over the temptation towards the object.

- If you can't make your dog give up items on command, ask your vet for a reliable animal behaviourist.

JUMPING UP

Dogs tend to jump up as a way of greeting people, especially if they weren't trained not to do this as a puppy. Jumping up can be a problem if out for a walk, especially if your dog approaches children or people who are afraid of dogs.

Try working hard on mastering the 'Sit' command and make sure you only reward with cuddles when the dog has all four feet on the ground, otherwise it will associate jumping up with praise. Begin this training as a puppy so it really sinks in.

If your dog does jump up to someone, tell the person to take a step back, turn around and completely ignore the dog, and to keep doing this until they lose interest. If the problem persists, keep your dog on a lead when it is around people until it learns to sit still.

CHEWING

Damage to furniture, shoes and other items caused by chewing can be very frustrating for dog owners.

Pocket fact ☙

Most dogs chew while they are in their adolescent stage, as they are essentially teething, waiting for their adult teeth to grow in.

While this is a normal stage which can last for about six months, chewing can be a sign of other problems such as:

- An unbalanced diet (the dog is trying to get more calcium)

- Seeking attention

- Distress or loneliness

- Boredom

Give your dog special chews (available from your vet or pet shop) and reward them for chewing these rather than the furniture. Make sure they don't have access to valuable items you don't want chewed and make sure they get plenty of exercise and you play with them regularly. You can even get a special bitter-tasting spray (usually available from vets) to discourage your dog from chewing the furniture.

CHASING CARS

Chasing cars can be very stressful for owners as there is the fear your dog could be injured or cause an accident.

This behaviour generally results from an instinctive herding behaviour and can, therefore, be difficult to combat. Your best bet is to keep an eye out for temptation while you are out with your dog and put it on the lead if you think it might start chasing. Try keeping your dog on the lead and exposing it to traffic (thereby removing the novelty and excitement) and reward it for paying attention to you rather than the cars.

BITING

Biting is a natural behaviour which most dogs learn to control by the time they are four months old. You must discourage all biting from an early age.

Puppies learn to inhibit their biting from their mother or from playing with other puppies (this is why socialisation is so crucial).

Puppies will learn that if they bite too hard their playmate will bite back or run away, teaching them about the force of their bite and why not to do it.

It is also critical that your dog socialises with people, especially people like the postman. Some dogs can develop phobias about certain kinds of people and can attack, so be sure to introduce your puppy to all sorts of people as often as possible.

If your puppy does bite you (and this can sometimes be play-biting) discourage the behaviour by responding forcefully, saying something like 'No' or 'Ouch' and ignoring the puppy until it behaves. Reward behaviours like licking instead.

Pocket tip

It is vital that you are confident your dog won't bite other people. If you can't be sure of this, keep the dog on its lead and consider hiring a professional trainer.

FIGHTING

Fighting between dogs can range from puppy playfights (where they learn to control their bite) to full-blown vicious battles between adult dogs.

Pocket tip

If there is a fight which needs breaking up, try to distract the dogs with loud noises rather than wading in physically. You don't want to get injured yourself.

While you should let puppies engage in playfights, it's vital that you learn to spot when things are getting too serious: if a puppy is trying to run away repeatedly it might be time to break things up.

Fights between adult dogs tend to result from young dogs taking on an older, dominant dog, or uncastrated male dogs. If you think your dog is likely to get in a fight keep it on the lead and watch its body language for signs of aggression. Also keep an eye out for any other dogs which may set it off.

Dog attacks

The Sun *reported that in 2008 nearly 5,000 people in the UK were hospitalised thanks to dogs. That's a rise of 50% since 1999.*

The Dangerous Dogs Act 1991 was a response to several dog attacks in the late 1980s and identified certain breeds as inherently dangerous. Legally, you can't keep a pure-bred Pit Bull Terrier (Staffordshire Bull Terriers are exempt) or a Japanese Tosa as a pet.

Many experts on canine behaviour have wondered how sensible or effective the law is, as labels such as 'dangerous' work only so far. Recently, Staffordshire Bull Terriers have come under fire for some notorious attacks on children. But many owners will say that they make for peaceful family pets on the whole. It seems that irresponsible dog owners and breeders are to blame.

A dog usually needs lots of negative training to attack someone. Dog attacks can stem from a variety of causes, ranging from fear to the territorial instinct to insatiable hunger for power.

To avoid getting bitten:

- A dog may try to get dominant over human members of its 'pack' by positioning itself where it's not supposed to, like a sofa or bed. Make it clear that this is unacceptable. If your dog shows continual signs of unwonted aggression, like snarling when you tell it get off a sofa – and basically refuses to get off – mention this to your vet on your next visit.

- Try not to step on a dog's tail or paw, or surprise a sleeping dog.

- If you must stop two dogs fighting, don't get involved physically and put yourself at risk of a bite.

- Don't stare at a dog you don't know well. This may feel threatening to the dog. Make sure that a child (who might be of the same height as the dog) doesn't stare either.

Pocket tip 🦴

Running away from a dog signals to the dog that you are weak, and this may trigger its predatory instincts.

- A fearful dog can interpret a hand extended towards its head by a stranger as an attempt at control. Unpleasant memories of harsh treatment might trigger a bite.

- Practise self-regulation exercises on your dog. Get your dog used to sudden movements and unexpected actions like moving the food bowl. This training will come in very useful in case your dog ever needs medical attention for an injury.

Make sure children don't anger a dog and make it bite:

- Ensure that a child does not tease a dog by pulling its ears or tail.

- Leave young children and dogs together without adult supervision only when you have a very well-mannered dog – and even then, avoid this situation as far as possible. Dogs are much more likely to attack children when an adult is not around. Remember, a child can't fend off an attacking dog like a strong adult could.

- Children sometimes go too close to a chained dog or try to touch a strange dog, which may not welcome such attention.

MUZZLES

Although there is a general idea that muzzles are cruel, they are useful in making sure your dog doesn't bite if it is in pain, such as when you try to examine an injury. It also prevents the dog from biting an infected area, restricts your dog if it has a tendency to fight with other dogs, and stops a dog from excessive barking and even from eating what it shouldn't.

What are the most common uses of a muzzle?

- It helps you walk a hyperactive dog in comfort.
- It helps when you bathe or groom a resistant dog.
- It helps you to put medicine in the dog's ear if there's an infection.

What kind of muzzle should you use?

- The Baskerville muzzle's open basket lets the dog breathe freely.
- You can also get muzzles made of lightweight fabrics such as nylon or mesh, which don't hinder the dog's movement.
- Don't use a muzzle that closes the dog's mouth completely and won't let it pant when it's hot (dogs can only sweat through the pads on their paws).
- Whatever muzzle you decide on, make sure it fits your dog's mouth properly. The bit across the nose should not rub over the eyes.

- Also make sure that the muzzle isn't loose, or else your dog can just shake it off.

- When fitting the muzzle, you will know the correct tightness when you can insert a small finger under the strap of the clasp around the neck.

How do you get your dog used to wearing the muzzle?

- Put their favourite sticky food (such as liver pâté or soft cheese) at the bottom of the muzzle and let the dog smell it. The dog will probably dip its snout into the muzzle, but don't try to fasten it now.

- Repeat this process a number of times, with lots of praise.

- After the dog is comfortable with the muzzle, fasten it but take it off immediately.

- Then, begin fastening it on for longer periods, but not at regular times or regular intervals.

Pocket tip

Try the muzzle on at various places, such as when you are cooking or when you're both in the park. Your dog will soon get used to it.

🐕 LOST DOGS 🐕

Man's best friend has a tendency to go missing at times; in fact 300,000 dogs go missing every year. What can you do to keep your family whole? A few don'ts to remember:

- Don't leave a dog alone in your car, or tied to a post while shopping.

- On a walk, don't let it off its lead unless you're absolutely sure it will run back to you when called.

- Don't leave your dog in the garden if you're going out.

When you and your dog are outside the house, as a responsible owner you should make sure your dog has a collar on. But collars can fall off or get damaged so there are a few steps you can take to make sure your dog is still identifiable.

MICROCHIPPING

Microchipping makes it easier to trace your dog in case it gets lost or is stolen.

To microchip your dog, contact your vet or local RSPCA branch. For a payment of £20, your dog will be implanted with a microchip tag.

The procedure is as simple as having an injection. The microchip is the size of a rice grain and is inserted into your dog's body in a painless operation. The microchip has its unique code number that goes on to the national PetLog database with the owner's details. So if your dog gets lost and is found by someone else, it can be identified through its code number on the microchip.

Pocket tip

After you've had your dog microchipped, remember to keep the identification number handy. A mobile phone may be the right place to store it.

Keep the contact number for PetLog (tel 0870 606 6751; www.petlog.org.uk) and those of your vet and the police handy.

If it ever happens that you do lose your dog, the microchip will certainly help. But don't forget the tried and tested routes as well — ask the postman, tell your vet, tell the police, and put up flyers everywhere.

And in case you ever find a lost canine roaming in your neighbourhood, tell the police if you can't see the owner's name on the tag. The police will get in touch with the local dog warden.

🐕 SEASONAL CONSIDERATIONS 🐈

Your dog, like you, needs certain kinds of care through the seasons.

WINTER CARE

- An outdoors dog needs more attention. A small shelter helps the dog keep warm and should be insulated from wind and water.

- It needs more food to cope with the frosts, and also enough fresh water throughout the day. You can use water bowls heated electrically, but keep changing the water.

- An indoors dog needs less overall attention, but keep a dog jacket handy for wet or cold weather. This applies especially to dogs with health problems, elderly dogs or dogs with short hair.

- When your dog comes indoors from the snow, remove ice, snow, salt and other de-icing particles from its toes and wipe its paws. Trapped moisture will damage the paws, and salt and de-icers may cause wounds. If there is danger of frostbite, don't rub the skin but take the dog to your vet.

- Don't let your dog taste anti-freeze. It tastes sweet and is poisonous to dogs, so if you know that your dog has lapped up any, go to the vet.

SUMMER CARE

- In the heat of summer, take your dog outdoors for exercise in the early morning before sunrise or in the evening after sunset.

Don't stay outdoors too long on very hot days, especially if it's humid.

Pocket tip 🦴

A dog's ears and nose can get sunburnt easily, and short-haired dogs are especially liable to sunburn all over.

- To avoid heatstroke, keep supplying your dog with lots of fresh, cool water.

- If you go travelling, take lots of drinking water and a towel. A wet towel will help the dog cool down quickly.

- Don't ever leave your dog in a car in hot weather. Cars can get hot enough to induce fatal heatstroke.

- Symptoms of heatstroke include staring or a stressed expression, lack of response to commands, excessive panting, dry and warm skin, high fever, dehydration, a rapid heartbeat and fainting. Dogs with existing heart problems, dogs used to colder climates, puppies and elderly dogs are particularly vulnerable. See your vet immediately if you spot any of these symptoms.

PUBLIC EVENTS

It can be tempting to take your dog to an event the whole family is attending, especially fairs and barbecues. However, there are a few key things you should consider first:

- Is the event dog friendly? Some public events don't allow dogs so make sure you check this first.

- Can you trust your dog off the lead, especially around other dogs and children? Even if your dog is usually well behaved bear in mind that all the extra noise and people will make it extra excitable.

- Feed your dog before you go so that it's not tempted by all the exciting food smells.

Make sure you bring plenty of water for your dog to drink and ensure you have the lead with you, just in case.

Events with fireworks

Fireworks can be very frightening for a dog and it's best to stay indoors during events like Guy Fawkes Night.

Most dogs will be anxious, especially those who have not been exposed to a variety of loud noises.

> *Pocket tip* 🦴
>
> *If you know there are going to be fireworks, take your dog for a walk during the day and keep him indoors while the fireworks are going off.*

- Don't leave the dog alone in the house and if it finds a place to hide (under the kitchen table for example) let it stay there where it feels safe.

- Shut the curtains and put on the TV or music at a high volume to drown out the sounds.

- Try feeding your dog a large meal (preferably carbohydrates) and it may feel sleepy.

- It is also possible to ask your vet for a diffuser which releases a dog-appeasing pheromone, which has a calming effect.

🐕 TRAVEL 🐕

Getting a dog used to changing environments is quite a task, but luckily dogs are very adaptable creatures.

MOVING HOUSE

While moving house for you can be an exciting prospect, for your dog it may mean a total uprooting from its beloved burrow. Dogs often get stressed out by the sheer sight of packed boxes and inverted furniture (their anxieties may include the fear that you will leave them behind).

- Consider leaving your dog with a family member or a friend, or with a dog-sitter or a boarding kennel, before you start packing the boxes.

- When you move into the new place, settle your dog's bed so that something feels familiar at least. Show it the basics, like where the food and water bowls will be kept, and where it should go to the loo. Let your dog wander around quietly so that it can take stock of its new environment.

LEAVING YOUR DOG WHILE YOU GO ON HOLIDAY

There are a number of places where your dog can stay when you go on holiday:

- Is there a family member or a friend whom your dog knows and likes? Leave your dog with its food, toys and bed at their home, together with your contact details and the vet's.

- Dogsitters may be found amongst students looking for part-time jobs – but make sure you know and trust the person. Try contacting the National Association of Registered Petsitters (tel 0845 2308544; www.dogsit.com). Do meet the dogsitter in advance, and check insurance liabilities and references. Leave your contact details and those of your vet.

- For boarding kennels, it's wise to visit the place beforehand and see the staff and arrangements for yourself. Friends or family may be able to recommend one, and lists of kennels can be found through the Animal Boarding Advice Bureau (tel 01606 891303).

Hotel for dogs

Nowadays instead of placing your dog in a kennel there is the option of putting your dog in a dog hotel. These luxury abodes have individual rooms and generally fewer dogs, meaning your pooch will receive more individual care and attention.

CHOOSING KENNELS

When trying to choose a boarding kennel for your dog make sure you do your research. Go on the internet or get advice from your vet. Visit a few kennels to make sure you get the one which is best for your dog.

While you're on your visit try to take note of things including:

● Does it smell clean?

● Is it very noisy?

● Is it clean and dry?

● Do the dogs look happy and healthy?

● Are the dogs allowed access to an outdoor area?

The owners should ask you for a vaccination certificate for your dog. You should also check that the kennel has a licence and ask what the policy is if your dog falls ill. Try to book as early as possible as kennels fill up fast and you don't want to miss out on your first choice.

When you drop your dog off make sure you leave your contact details and the details of your vet. Expect to pay something like £15 to £50 daily.

TRAVELLING WITH YOUR DOG

Pet Passports

The Pet Travel Insurance Scheme (helpline 0870 241 1710) lets you take a dog to certain countries without quarantine, subject to some conditions. This list and the conditions are updated periodically, so check at Defra (Department for Environment, Food and Rural Affairs) www.defra.gov.uk.

Onwers must have their animal microchipped, vaccinated against rabies and blood tested in order to obtain a 'pet passport' and travel under this scheme.

Things to take care of before you travel:

- Is your dog on pet insurance?

- It can take six months or more for a pet passport application to be processed so make sure you leave enough time to arrange this.

- Is your dog microchipped for identification?

- Check with your vet about vaccinations. Your dog should be vaccinated against rabies. On the certificate, make sure you have the following details:

    Date of birth

    The microchip identification number

Date of vaccination

Type of vaccination, with the product name and the batch

Date of booster vaccination

ON THE MOVE

A puppy used to travelling by car will usually grow into a happy travelling dog. Many airline companies nowadays are willing to accommodate a pet – check with the company for their requirements.

Essentials to remember:

- Pack water bottles with your dog's water bowl. A panting dog can get dehydrated easily, so keep replenishing the water supply. You may also need to carry food and food bowls, depending on how long you travel for.

- Pack plastic bags to clean up dog mess – it's one of the key responsibilities of dog owners, and you may be fined if you ignore it.

- Get a dog carrier, and get your dog used to it before you travel by padding it with nice bedding and a treat. Make sure the bedding is absorbent, in case the flight or train is delayed or the travel period is long. See that the carrier has enough ventilation. Check with the train or airline company about the carrier size.

- Arrange your dog's stay at the destination. For foreign travel, many countries require a quarantine period when you arrive. If this is not required, make sure that that the place you are staying will welcome a doggy guest.

4

A DOG'S LIFE

Just like humans, your dog will need different kinds of care from birth through to old age.

🐕 THE PUPPY 🐕

When you have a new puppy arriving in your home for the very first time, there are a few essentials you will need:

- Puppy food
- Food bowls and water bowls
- Toys, including chewing toys made of rawhide
- Toothbrush and toothpaste
- Nail clippers
- Brushes and comb
- Lead and collar
- Kennel and bedding

MAKING A PUPPY WELCOME

- Make a plan. Who will feed the puppy? Who will clean up? Who will keep an eye on the lonely puppy at night?

- What are the restricted areas for the puppy? Close off that room where you don't want a wandering puppy — and make sure the bathroom doors stay closed when your new family member arrives.

- Move fragile objects, small toys and remote controls out of the puppy's reach.

- Keep household plants and cleaners out of bounds, and tape together any dangling electrical wires.

The crate

Rather than thinking of your puppy's crate as merely a crate, try to think of it as a den instead. It's a good idea to start your puppy off in a crate; it gives it a safe place of its own and will help it adjust to its new surroundings.

The crate can be made of wire or fibreglass, and should be just large enough for the puppy to lie down in comfort. If your puppy is a large breed and you'd rather not keep buying new crates as it grows, buy a large crate and then partition it for the puppy.

How is the crate useful?

- **Rest and refuge.** If you need to leave the house for a while, leave the pup in the crate so that it won't wander around and chew up your shoes. And if it does behave badly in your absence, then send it back to the crate. It will get the message that the crate can become a cage when it's been naughty. Just make sure that the puppy has plenty of open space and exercise when it has been good.

Pocket tip 🦴

Pups often take to sleeping in the crate of their own will. If there are children in the house, keep a blanket over the crate so they know not to disturb the pup. And if your pup is scared at night, move the crate close to your bed instead of cradling it in your arms. Otherwise you'll end up with a dog who won't ever desert your bed.

- **Food.** The crate is a space where your puppy can eat in peace, and the limited space ensures that it won't run around right after its meal and have issues with its digestion.

- **Housetraining.** For a puppy which still wets or soils its bed, in addition to dog nappies you can use Vetbed, bedding which stays dry on the surface. Avoid shredded paper unless you change it at least once a day. Once you start training the puppy by sending it outdoors, you have to live with an occasionally recalcitrant puppy which may think that its crate houses a loo.

THE NEWBORN PUPPY

If you are buying a puppy, you will probably take ownership of your new dog at around seven weeks. See p.77 for more on where to buy puppies from and what to look for.

Pocket fact 🐾

A puppy is toothless, deaf and blind at its birth, and its eyes open after two weeks. Until the age of four weeks, its care is very much the province of its mother.

If it happens that you're in charge of a newborn puppy, remember that the usual age to wean the puppy from the mother's milk is when it's four weeks old. The milk teeth will begin to appear at this time. If you have more than one puppy, once the puppies have been weaned, feed them separately.

Don't overfeed a puppy just to make it grow faster. A puppy that has been pushed out of its youth may develop other problems like hip dysplasia, which will impair it its whole life.

The puppy needs to get comfortable around people, so handle it gently. The correct way to hold a puppy is with one hand under the chest and the other supporting the rear end. Holding it next to your chest will make your puppy feel secure and relax in your arms. Beware of picking up puppies by their legs, tail or neck as this can cause serious bone or nerve damage to a puppy's tender body.

Pocket tip 🦴

On your journey home with your new puppy, ensure someone is in charge of holding it — so it is both secure and safe.

FOUR TO SEVEN WEEKS

- When the puppy is four to five weeks old, the mother will become less watchful over her young ones. It's time to give them toys to play with.

- At five weeks they are old enough to spend some time out-doors every day, under supervision.

- A puppy will usually be around seven weeks old when it arrives at your home.

Play

Play with the puppy, but don't spend too much time with it. The puppy needs a lot of sleep at this time, so make sure people respect that.

Food

The puppy has been weaned by now and is very hungry for solid food. Feed the puppy four times a day. Keep reducing the feeds over time – it will need a meal at least three times a day until it's four months old, and only two as an adult dog. You can serve the puppy's meals in the crate, at fixed times. Don't leave the food out indefinitely – let your puppy eat for 15 minutes, then take the bowl away.

Always have clean and fresh drinking water available for your puppy. Do change the water after every feed.

Pocket fact ❧

Growing puppies need extra calcium, and some owners add this to their diet in the form of bone meal. But this must be done only after you've talked to your vet, because the amount of calcium must be proportionate to the phosphorus and magnesium in the puppy's diet. Too much calcium can be bad for your puppy.

Housetraining

After every meal or nap, take the puppy outdoors so that it can relieve itself. Stay outdoors for about 10 minutes, and if the puppy hasn't obliged, bring it back indoors, put it in the crate, and don't play with it. Take it outdoors again after 10–15 minutes, and keep repeating the routine until the puppy gets it. Play with it and give it hugs only after it's got the idea. Housetraining is a bit labour-intensive at the beginning, but most dogs are clever enough to learn that where you live isn't where you mess.

Vaccinations

Your puppy's vaccinations will usually start at six to eight weeks of age, and continue every three or four weeks until it is 16 weeks old.

Some puppies can have a vaccine reaction, in the form of a mild fever and muscle ache. In this case the puppy will have a lack of appetite and sleep for 24–48 hours. Other puppies may have a more serious reaction as they vomit or have swellings on the face. This can be taken care of for further vaccinations with anti-allergy medication like an antihistamine. Don't skip the vaccinations, but do alert your vet for future reference.

EIGHT TO 12 WEEKS

The puppy will still sleep a lot at this stage and will also mature rapidly, waking up to the world. It will explore its surroundings excitedly, and dart about restlessly. Its sense of smell will be very acute and it will sniff at anything and everything.

The first command

This is a good time to teach your puppy the training command 'Come' (other training commands can be saved for later, see p.126). This command is technically known as the 'recall' and is very important when you take your older puppy out to public places.

Socialising

Children should be encouraged to play with the puppy – caring for it is now the whole family's job. Socialising is very important at this stage as an overprotected puppy will grow up to be a fearful adult.

It's important to get the puppy used to human touch.

- Over the course of every day, pick up the puppy and lie on the floor with it or place it in your lap. Even if it struggles to run away, don't relent.

- Rub its tummy and talk until it relaxes.

- Scratch its back and wiggle its ears, like a massage. The puppy might nip back at you, but make it clear that you're the one in control. Let the whole family play with the puppy in this way.

Throughout its life your dog will have to encounter the touch of people – be it at the vet's or at the groomer's or at the boarding kennels. It has to get comfortable with being handled by strangers.

Pocket tip ✔

Exploring the world may involve walking into its traps. The puppy will occasionally get scared of the unfamiliar and you will then see its hackles rise. A stressed puppy needs your comfort.

Housetraining

A puppy needs not to get stressed by your rules. Continue the housetraining as before.

Grooming

A puppy does not need to be fully groomed or bathed until it's at least a year old. This is to preserve the natural oils in its skin.

Clip the puppy's nails once a week. A soft brushing, followed by a gentle rubbing with a damp towel or flannel, will be sufficient for hygiene.

During these sessions, keep massaging the puppy and keep talking in a soothing voice. This will help you have a dog that looks forward to being groomed and bathed.

12 TO 16 WEEKS

The puppy's exploration of the world will now be accomplished through its mouth, as its first permanent teeth emerge. This will continue until it is seven months old and has all 42 of its teeth.

Chewing

Provide good quality chewing toys for your teething puppy, unless you want the house covered in foam from your bed or sofa. At the same time, make it clear that the bed and the sofa are not to be chewed, and nor are human body parts.

Who's the boss

As the puppy grows into independence, it might try out the role of a pack leader and challenge you. Be unyielding and show it who is boss. Cute puppy behaviour can grow into unforgiveable dog behaviour.

A collar

You will be spending more time outdoors at this point, and you'll have a lively puppy on your hands. To avert the danger of it running away, do invest in a collar (with a name tag) and a lead, and consider a microchip.

FOUR TO EIGHT MONTHS

Exercise

- As you spend more time outdoors with your puppy, start with a slow, short walk in the neighbourhood, and then gradually increase the speed and length of your walks.

- Make sure not to over-exercise the puppy though – dogs' bones do not fully develop until they are 18 months old.

- Gentle play is fine for a puppy, but avoid long jumps and high jumps which will stress its soft bones, muscles and ligaments.

- Keep an eye on your puppy when it plays with an adult dog, as it will keep playing non-stop until it's too tired to get up any more.

- Your puppy will have grown ever more confident. It will show interest in chasing other animals, so keep a good grip on the lead, only taking it off the lead in an enclosed area.

Behavioural training

As the puppy asserts itself, it might start growling if a child approaches. Don't allow bad behaviour to prevail – the first six months of a puppy's life are crucial in shaping its relationship to the family.

Socialising

Get your dog used to family visitors. When a friend visits, have him or her give the puppy a biscuit. The puppy will learn that strangers whom the family likes are to be welcomed and not to be jumped up at or barked at.

EIGHT MONTHS TO A YEAR

The puppy is now about half to three-quarters of its adult size. Females will have reached their ultimate height, but will continue to grow in breadth.

Spay or neuter your puppy, if that's your long-term plan. Some dogs are sexually mature by the time they are eight months old.

Food

Reduce the feeding frequency to three or even two meals over the day.

Training

Your puppy is now old enough to begin an obedience training programme in earnest. See p.126 for training methods.

🐕 ADOLESCENT DOGS 🐕

Now you have an adult dog, with some teenage giddiness but also a sense of adult responsibility and maturity.

Just like humans, dogs go through a phase when they shoot up into adulthood, and the transition can be quite uncomfortable. When your dog will experience this depends on the breed, but it will be roughly between six to 18 months of age.

The marks of doggy adolescence

- **Chewing everything to bits**. The permanent teeth are coming in now, so make sure you have enough chew toys around. If your dog doesn't chew, it may be troubled later with dental problems, so do be a little less annoyed at your dog for ripping the sofa open just now.

- **Growing pains**. Not much you can do about this, but your vet might prescribe something helpful.

- **Your dog might be horny**. Males will be aggressive towards other male dogs. The intact female dog experiences its first heat cycle. You will see it flirting with male dogs, and being aggressive towards other female dogs.

- **Dog fights**. The intact male dog produces a lot more testosterone now than it will as an adult, so you will see it spraying its territory, wandering and dog asserting itself within the 'pack' of other dogs it socialises with. This is likely to result in some tussles.

Biting

As your adolescent dog tries to establish a dominant position in its pack (consisting of other dogs as well as members of its human family), biting can become a problem.

Biting by a puppy under the age of six months can be easily corrected. A puppy's bite generally won't hurt, and people often dismiss it as cute. This is the mistake – never let your puppy acquire a taste for human flesh! Or, for that matter, kitten flesh or other pets in the house.

A year-old dog, whose puppy biting habits are uncorrected, will start 'play biting', where it will test out how far it can go, and how much you will bend as pack leader. This behaviour can still be modified through obedience training.

> *Pocket tip* 🦴
>
> *If you can't correct biting tendencies at this early stage, you may end up facing an adult dog you can't trust not to bite other animals or people.*

Help for a skittish adolescent dog

- Sometimes you can't be sure whether your dog's behaviour is just a phase that will pass, or whether it's here to stay. If you've got your dog from a breeder, ask if the behaviour is normal for the dog's breed and bloodline.

- Your dog's adolescence will go in fits and starts. Sometimes it will have matured a lot in two months, and sometimes you won't see much change in its behaviour. Females will usually mature faster than males.

- You need to keep reinforcing the obedience training that you gave when it was a puppy.

- While a puppy seems to love anything in human shape, an adolescent will develop likes and dislikes. It will be nice to develop that special bond with your dog, but make sure it doesn't turn into a 'one-master dog' at this stage. You will regret it later if you have to go travelling and leave your dog with a dog-sitter.

- Stay patient with your dog. Remember, your adolescent has the excited brain of a puppy in an adult's body. Sad but true – this is the time when owners may give up and hand their dogs over to the rescue shelter. Bide your time, and you may well be rewarded with a best friend.

Outdoors or indoors?

In the past, many dogs, especially working dogs, used to live in outdoor kennels. Now, many people prefer to keep dogs indoors, and a lot of rescue shelters won't let you adopt a dog if you keep it outdoors.

It's hard to make a blanket policy on keeping a dog outdoors or indoors. Dogs with a working ancestry, like Border Collies, seem happy with a home on the moor as long as it's well-insulated from cold winds. Many people keep an outdoor kennel in their garden for dogs who actually live indoors. There are uses for a doggy outbuilding:

- *It makes a den for your dog which its own kingdom – provided that it doesn't have to fight over space with another dog, if you have more than one.*
- *It's a good place to dismiss your dogs to when you have visitors who don't care for them.*

🐕 ELDERLY DOGS 🐕

Your dog can live into a happy and healthy old age with a few lifestyle adjustments. In fact it can be nicer to have an older dog around – they won't demand a 10-mile walk, and will be happy to sit quietly with you in the garden instead.

It's hard to tell when exactly a dog becomes a senior citizen, because this varies from dog to dog depending on main factors:

- **Its size and breed**. Small dogs usually live longer. Turn to p.10 for a chart showing the average lifespan of different breeds.

- **Its lifestyle**. General health, diet and exercise all play a role in determining how long a dog will live.

Signs of ageing

The best way to know when your dog is getting old is simply to observe. Look out for the following signs (dogs may show only a few of these symptoms, but it will be time for you to make some changes to your dog's daily routine):

- Your dog may become less energetic. Its joints may get stiff and it may take time to get up when it has been sitting or lying down.

- The coat may get a coarser texture, and hair may be shed. You might even see white hair.

- It might not respond when you call it – this may be deafness.

- Dental problems may develop. Your dog might have difficulty eating as food drops out its mouth, or it salivates excessively. If you see swellings below its eye, there may be a tooth abscess that needs the vet's attention.

- Its eyes might develop a blue tinge, which may be harmless. If the tinge is white there may be a cataract which needs attention from your vet, otherwise blindness will develop.

- Look out for warts and lumps. These may be cancerous, but treated in time, can cause your dog much less pain.

- Your dog might be thirsty or need to go outdoors to the loo frequently.

- It can have bouts of memory loss when it can't recognise its surroundings.

- It might have a loss of appetite.

Pocket fact 🐾

Generally, a very old dog will get thin and its ribs will stick out — but some dogs may gain weight.

- It may sleep more in the day and be sleepless at night.

- It may have moods, get snappy and destroy household objects.

Help in the later years

- See the vet regularly for check-ups, and report anything unusual.

- Your dog still needs exercise despite its possible unwillingness. Older dogs frequently suffer from arthritis or obesity.

- Apart from your regular grooming and bathing, you might want your dog to see a professional groomer more often.

- Keep checking your dog's teeth and gums for dental health.

- Your dog will need low-calorie foods now, with easily digestible high-quality protein, and plenty of vitamins and minerals. You will find special food for older dogs at the pet shop. Your dog might also prefer to have lighter, but more frequent meals as opposed to the two big meals it has been used to.

- Finally, be patient with your occasionally snappy dog. It's difficult for it not to be able to do the exciting jumps and runs it used to. Your support could make all the difference to its last years.

🐕 HAVING A DOG PUT DOWN 🐕

*'You think dogs will not be in heaven? I tell you, they will
be there long before any of us.'*
Robert Louis Stevenson

It may be that your old dog is suffering so much that it makes
sense to put it down. It's usually up to the owner to decide when
the dog's quality of life has become so bad that it is kinder to put
it out of its misery.

Most vets will put a dog to sleep through a lethal injection that
brings on a calm, painless and dignified passing. There are other
options, such as the injection of a substance called T-61 which
causes paralysis and some pain (and the old-fashioned method of
shooting the dog). By far, the first method is most commonly used
in the UK.

It's a big and painful decision to willingly have your dog put to
sleep, and it's natural to grieve. If you find the grief too hard
to bear, there are counselling services that can help you come to
terms with loss. You can work through bereavement by getting in
touch with the animal charity Blue Cross (tel 01993 822651;
www.bluecross.org.uk).

QUICK TIPS
ON OWNING A DOG

- Carefully consider the cost and time you will need to commit to different breeds before choosing your puppy.

- Make your lifestyle suits your dog and not the other way around.

- Choose a reputable breeder or shelter to get your dog from.

- Have your puppy's routine and your home ready before your puppy arrives.

- Make sure you have a vet and pet insurance lined up.

- Make sure you have all the equipment you need before your puppy arrives home: crate, bedding, bowls, lead, brush, toys, ID collar.

- Make sure you know how to groom your dog properly: do they have a silky, long, short or smooth coat?

- Practise trimming their nails and brushing their teeth while they are a puppy. This will make things much easier when they are an adult.

- Start training your puppy as soon as it arrives: especially its name and toilet habits.

- Use food treats and a clicker to train your puppy.

- Try to socialise your puppy from a young age so that it doesn't become an aggressive or anxious adult.

- Know how to deal with mishaps and any other problem behaviour like biting or possessive aggression.

- Consider whether you want to have your dog microchipped in case it gets lost.

- Make sure you set up a regular dental routine to care for their teeth. You can use a dog's teeth to tell how old they are.

- Make sure they get enough exercise appropriate to their size and age. This includes both walks and games.

- Make sure you monitor their health; such as their weight, any signs of illness or infestations.

- Learn to understand your dog's barks and body language so you know what they are trying to tell you.

- Take time to introduce other family members such as other pets, children and strangers.

- Consider your dog's different needs depending on the season or if you are attending a public event.

- Make kennel or travel arrangements (such as a pet passport) well in advance.

- Know how to care for your dog at different stages of its life.

- Have fun with your dog. Dogs are loyal and lovable pets: make sure you enjoy owning one!

DOG TERMINOLOGY

Here are some definitions for a few basic doggy terms you may come across.

Alpha: the dog of the highest ranking or dominance in a pack or group.

Bitch: a female dog.

Bloodline: line of pedigree and descent.

Dam: the female dog chosen for breeding, the mother of the litter.

Dealer: one who buys and sells dogs bred by others.

Docking: to cut or clip a dog's tail.

Dominance: assertive characteristics of a dog and its influence over other dogs.

High in rear: a dog that is higher over its rear quarters than over its front quarters.

High-stationed: tall and long-legged.

In and In: inbreeding of dogs without regard to results.

Litter: a group of puppies born at one time.

Mongrel: dog resulting from cross-breeding, between parents of different breeds.

Pedigree: dog with a recorded genealogy.

Racy: long-legged with a slight build.

Rangy: long-bodied with a shallow chest.

Schutzhund: a sport that started in Germany, which trains dogs to a very high level, often for guard and attack work and sometimes for competition.

Sire: the male dog chosen for breeding purposes, the father of a litter of pedigree puppies.

Square-proportioned: height at withers equal to length from point of sternum to point of croup.

Whelping: the process of puppies being born.

USEFUL CONTACTS

The Kennel Club

www.thekennelclub.org.uk
0870 606 6750

Dogs Trust

www.dogstrust.org.uk
020 7837 0006

RSPCA

www.rspca.org.uk
Advice line: 0300 1234 555

PetLog

0870 606 6751
www.petlog.org.uk

National Association of Registered Petsitters

www.dogsit.com
0845 2308544

Animal Boarding Advice Bureau

01606 891303

Kennel Directory

www.kenneldirectory.com
08700 114 115

Association of Pet Dog Trainers

www.apdt.co.uk
01285 810811

Centre of Applied Pet Ethology

www.coape.org
0800 783 0817

Blue Cross

www.bluecross.org.uk
01993 822651

INDEX

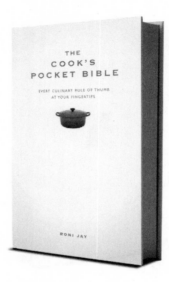